You Can Be The Bank

By
Todd Corbin

LEGAL NOTICE:

The You Can Be The Bank is a trademark of Conner Marketing Group Inc.

Neither the author nor their companies, in any way make any warranty, guaranty or representation, expressed or implied, as to the potential volume, profits, or success of any activity or undertaking described herein. All information related to the potential to earn money or realize a profit from any activity described herein was received from third parties and was not created or verified by the authors or any agent of either of them.

This publication is not intended and should not be used or construed as an offer to sell, or a solicitation of any offer to buy, securities of any fund or other investment product in any jurisdiction. No such offer or solicitation may be made prior to the delivery of definitive offering documentation.

This information within is designed to provide competent and reliable information regarding the subject matter covered. However, it is sold with the understanding that the author and publisher are not engaged in rendering legal, financial, or other professional advice. Laws and practices often vary from state to state and country to country and if legal or other expert assistance is required, the services of a professional should be sought. The authors specifically disclaim any liability that is incurred from the use or application of the contents of this book. The reader should conduct an independent investigation into the information contained herein before taking any action.

Visit my website at: https://integrityinvestsolutions.com

ISBN: 9798863335148

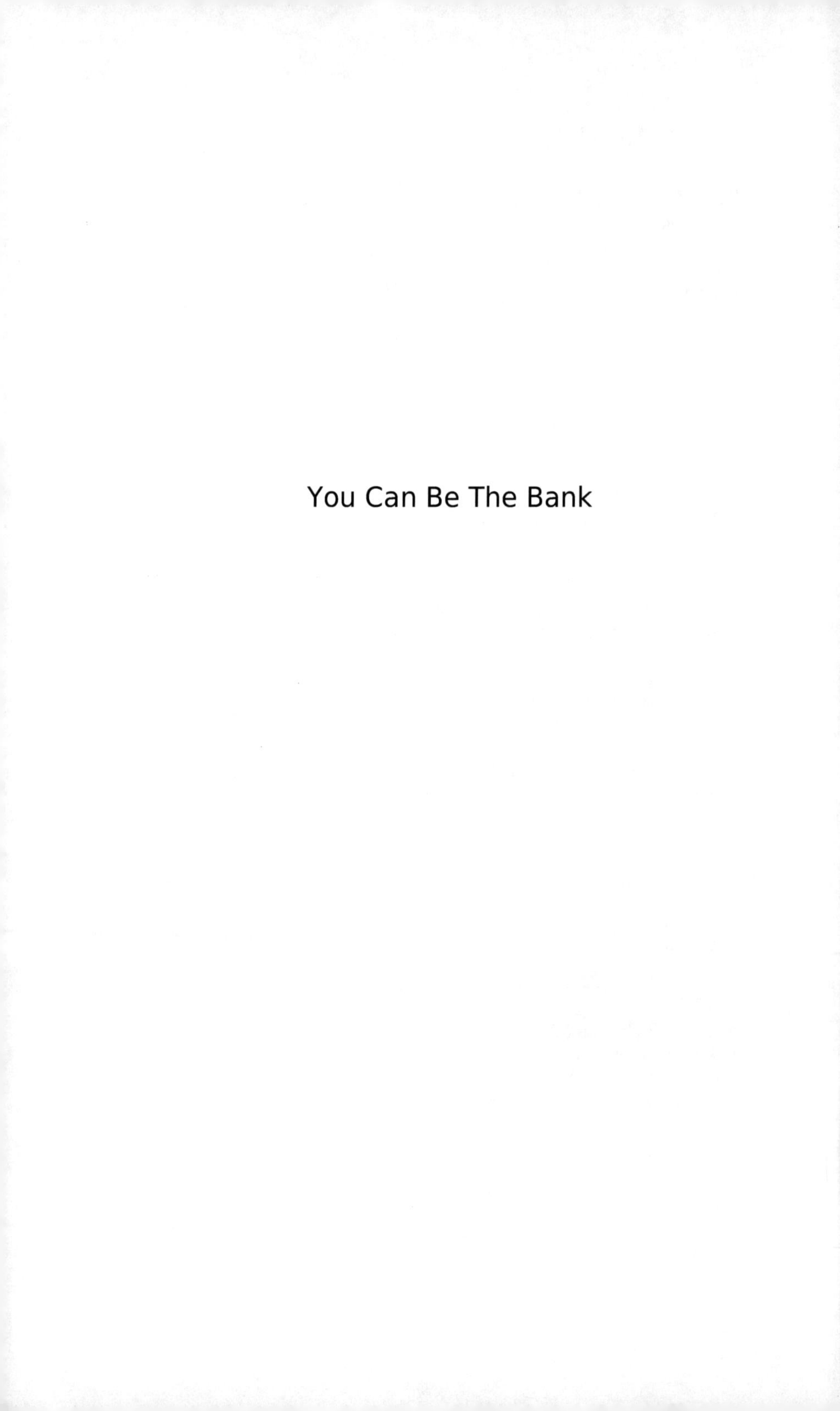

You Can Be The Bank

Free! – Special Bonus Gift

As my way of saying thank you for taking an active role in your success education, I have made an additional bonus gift available to you worth over $97, and it's yours absolutely free for picking up You Can Be The Bank!

Visit my special book bonus website and get your special report called How To Use Your Self-Directed IRA To Unlock Unlimited Tax-Free or Tax-Deferred Earnings.

This special report will walk you through step-by-step on how to become a private lender using your Traditional or ROTH IRA and multiply your earnings safely and securely.

Get it here:
https://integrityinvestsolutions.com/#freereport

As an added bonus, when you get the report, I'll send you an invitation to attend Jay Conner's upcoming 3-Day Private Money Conference priced at $2,997 per person.

When you attend, you'll learn exactly what I do and why I do it. You'll see for yourself how safe and secure your money will be when you work with me as a private lender. Jay's attorney will be at this event along with some of his existing private lenders! You will be able to see exactly how private lending works and how you can earn money on your money safely and securely. As my guest, the ticket price of $2,997 is waived, and you can now attend for only a $97 registration fee for both YOU and a guest!

Thank you and I hope you enjoy reading the book!

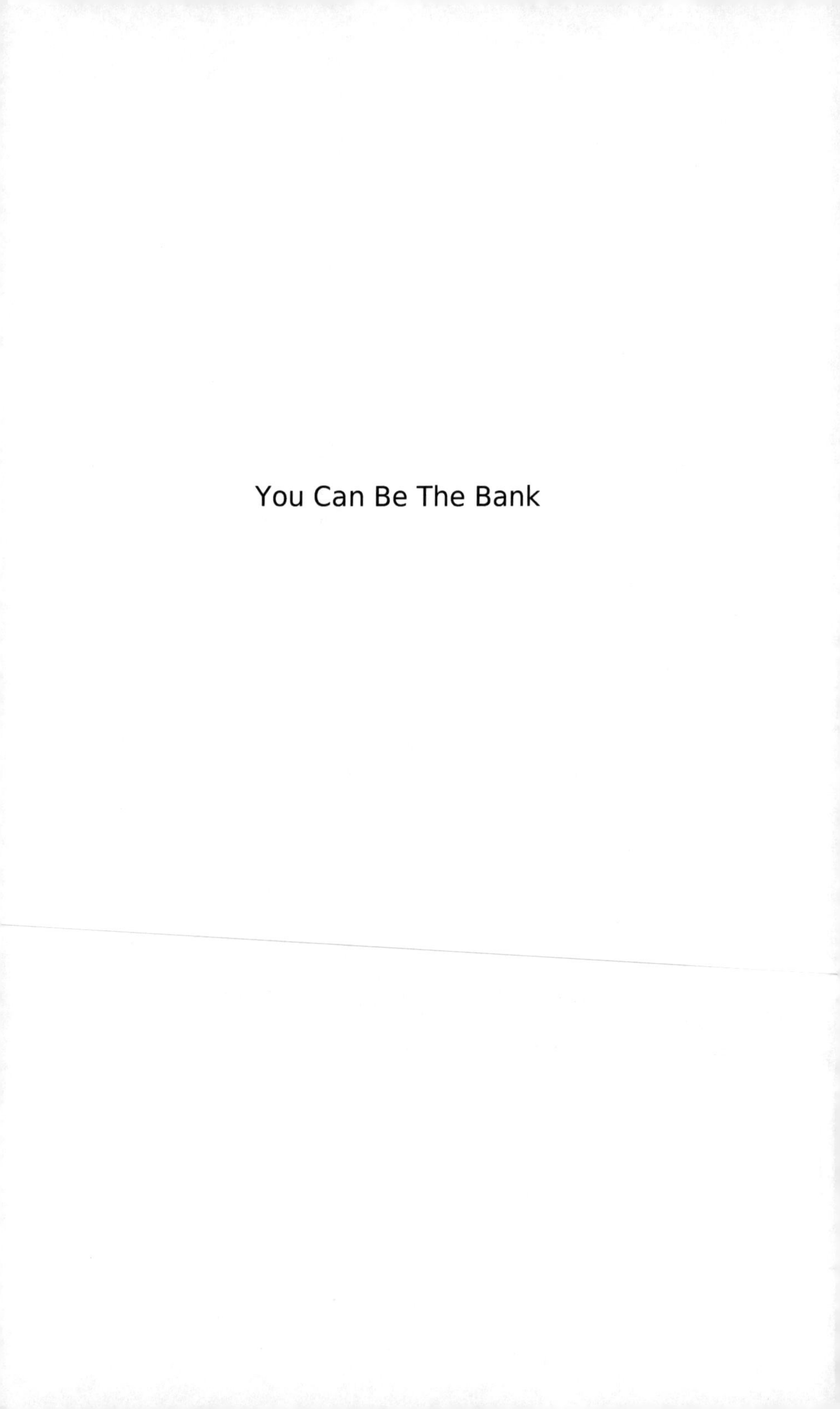

You Can Be The Bank

DEDICATION

This book is dedicated to my wife, Liana Corbin, who has been my biggest cheerleader; my voice of reason; and my behind-the-scenes miracle worker.

She is the love of my life, my best friend, and my loyal partner, no matter what storms come our way.

Our road has not been an easy one, but through it all, you have been there for me.

You are a gift from God to me. He really knew what He was doing when He made you. You are exactly the person I needed, and I will always love you.

You Can Be The Bank

ACKNOWLEDGMENTS

I would like to acknowledge Jay Conner, the Private Money Authority, for teaching me how to work with private lenders and to approach business with a servant's heart. Jay and his wife, Carol Joy, certainly live what they preach.

They serve with such humility and integrity, and have walked with me and so many others in this pathway to financial freedom. I am humbled and honored to know them and work with them.

I also would like to acknowledge a few others who have held my hand as I went from a life that had only known ministry to seeing how being in business can also transform the lives of many. That was important to me as I never want to stop helping people.

Thank you, Crystal Baker, Chaffee-Thanh Nguyen, and Eric and Erica Camardelle for all the wisdom and advice you have imparted to me through this journey, and for cheering me on when I was hit with trials. I couldn't be where I am today without any of the people in this acknowledgement.

FOREWORD
By Jay Conner

In the aftermath of the housing crash in 2008, I found myself at the forefront of reshaping real estate investment dynamics. My mission was clear: to establish a system where real estate investors could collaborate with private lenders, not just to protect their funds but also to extend a helping hand to homeowners in distress. This system, which has been the backbone of my own business, has successfully facilitated over 475 real estate deals, raising millions of dollars. It's a pleasure to contribute this foreword to Todd Corbin's groundbreaking book, "You Can Be The Bank."

As "The Private Money Authority," my journey has been one of continuous learning and sharing, and in the process, I've had the privilege of getting to know Todd over the past two years. Todd's commitment to integrity and his genuine concern for his business colleagues and private lenders set him apart in an industry that sometimes lacks such virtues. As an active member of my real estate investing mastermind community, Todd embodies the essence of a true "Go-Giver," ensuring that every transaction creates a multitude of winners.

Beyond his business prowess, Todd's involvement in mission work is a testament to his servant's heart. His desire to make a positive impact is not confined to his business dealings but extends to every sphere of his life.

In my role as a coach, I've closely observed Todd's professionalism when working with his private lenders. He not only follows my step-by-step Private Money system diligently but also imparts this knowledge to new private lenders. Todd's commitment to mastering and teaching this system places him among my top elite Mastermind Members, making me genuinely excited for you to delve into the world of private lending through Todd Corbin's perspective.

In "You Can Be The Bank," Todd shares the comprehensive guide to becoming a private lender. Each chapter is a treasure trove of knowledge, providing you with a step-by-step approach to safeguarding your assets and making informed investment decisions. Todd's ability to make complex concepts easy to understand is not just commendable—it's transformative. By the time you finish this book, you'll wonder why you hadn't encountered Todd's insights sooner.

I'm genuinely thrilled for you as you embark on this journey with Todd Corbin. May your venture into private lending be as rewarding and impactful as Todd's own experiences. Welcome to a world where financial wisdom meets genuine, positive change!

Jay Conner

Table Of Contents

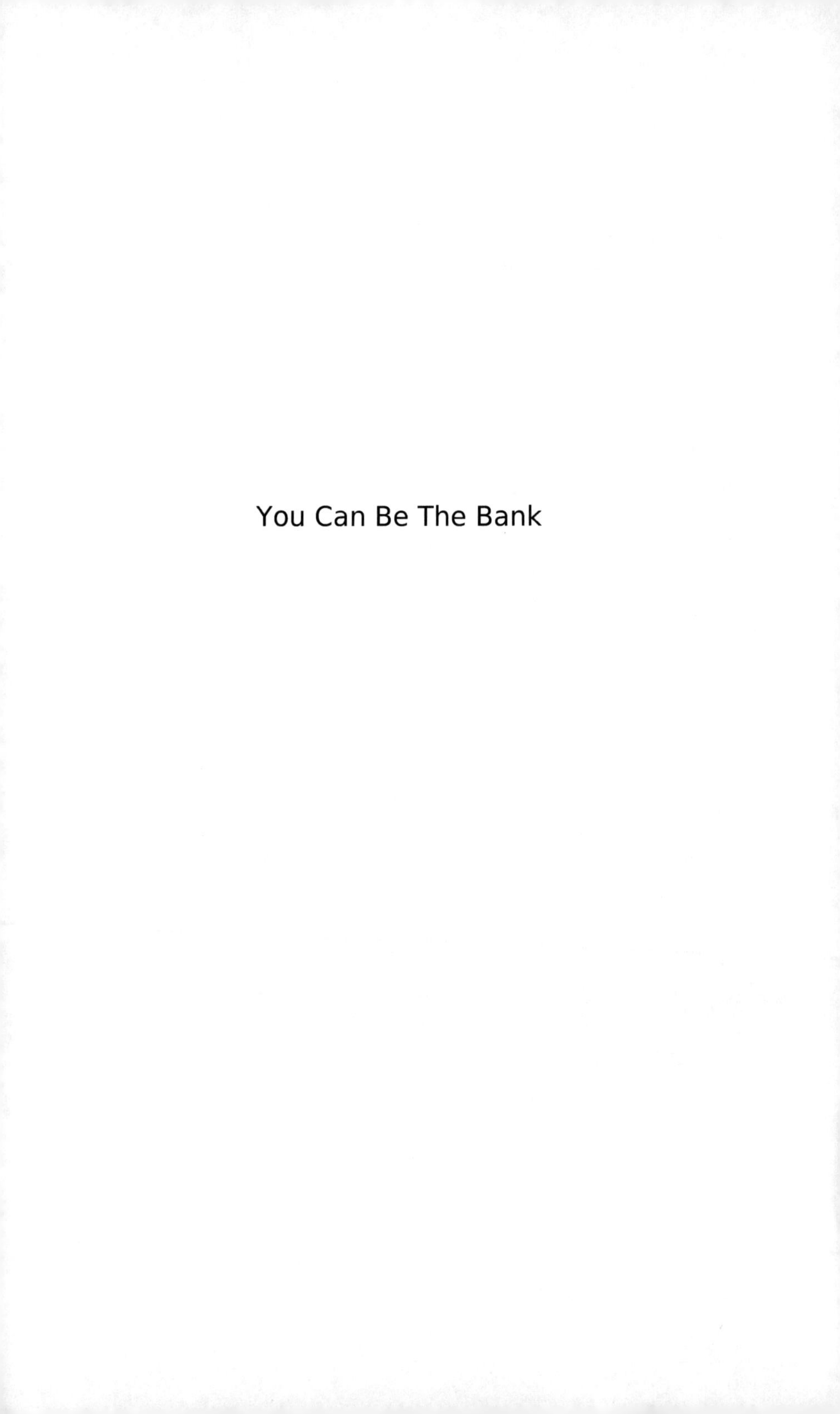

You Can Be The Bank

"Let your mind dance with me. Let it be, just for a moment, stress free."
-- Debasish Mridha

Your Introduction To Stress Free Investing

Thank you for getting a copy of The Magic Of Private Lending! Inside this book, you'll discover a great way to earn high rates of return safely and securely in a way that most folks don't even know exists.

With this information, you can significantly increase the value of any investment capital you or your IRA currently has in a CD, money market account, mutual fund, commodities, the stock market, or anything else.

This book will help you create wealth with passive investments secured by real estate for a safe and very attractive return.

Most people try to generate retirement income by following conventional wisdom and letting other people control their money and make the decisions for them. But, unfortunately, by the time they need the money, they discover they have barely kept up with inflation, and the cost of living has risen faster than their investments.

Take, for example, Mike.

Mike and his wife have been happily married with three kids for almost 30 years. Both of them have been working at the same companies for over 25 years each!

He is 57 years old, and she is 55 years old. They want to retire within five years to enjoy their golden years. One day, as he was thinking about retirement, Mike had an epiphany.

If he worked another eight years until he was 65 years old, commonly referred to as "retirement age," then he and his wife might only have another 15 - 20 years or so to enjoy their time together if they were perfectly healthy.

It dawned on him that most people work most of their lives and only get to enjoy a short period of it when they decide to retire – if they're lucky. And while he'd be able to retire in 8 years, he'd still have to constantly monitor his finances to ensure that there's enough money at the end of the month since he won't be working anymore.

Mike knew that when he actually did retire, he wanted to relax and not worry about finances. In addition, he and his wife wanted to purchase a lovely home on the beach where they could spend the rest of their lives.

Unfortunately for Mike, if he does purchase a new home on the beach, he will still have to continue working to continue his current lifestyle.

Then he learned about what will be discussed in detail in this book... the world of Private Lending.

Taking his newfound knowledge, Mike decided to become a Private Lender.

Working with the right people and becoming a private lender now, Mike will be able to purchase his dream home on the beach in 8 years and retire as planned - without having to worry about his finances.

To be clear, this is not a get-rich-quick scheme or strategy.

Mike will not be able to retire immediately using this technique. It won't make him a multi-millionaire in any short period of time. As mentioned, it was part of an 8-year (and beyond) plan.

What this strategy of being a private lender does, though, is allow him to enjoy his golden years. He can purchase the home of his dreams with his wife of almost 30 years, and they can feel financially secure knowing that his investments are growing quickly, while being safe and secure! In addition, he won't have to worry about continuing to work a 9-to-5 job to pay the bills, and as a bonus, his wife can also retire at the same time!

What you're going to learn in this book is not about conventional wisdom. It's been proven that the super-wealthy person who earned their wealth does not live by conventional wisdom.

And, if you want to enjoy the fruits of your labor, you will have to forego conventional wisdom as well.

Otherwise, if you do things like everyone else, you'll have to be satisfied with the low returns that following the herd mentality produces.

The good news is... you no longer have to accept low rates of return.

You are reading this book, so you can consider joining forces with me to create a mutually beneficial and profitable relationship.

And when you implement what is discussed in this book, you don't have to watch the stock market, call your broker, or wait for the next crash.

Using this strategy, instead of earning less than 1% on a savings account or Certificate of Deposit (CD), you can be the bank!

You can earn high rates of return safely and securely because your investment is always secured with a Deed of Trust on a property.

So, how do you do this?

How can you achieve low risk and high returns without worrying about stock market fluctuations?

It's simple.

You can achieve this all through the power of private lending!

Being a Private Lender can be a very lucrative investment vehicle for you for many reasons.

First is the safety issue.

When you work with me, barring specific circumstances, I don't allow my private lenders to invest more than 75% of the after-repaired value of a property.

I'll go into a lot more detail on this later in the book, and for now, know that in case I lose my mind, you, as my private lender, are left with a huge amount of equity as a safety cushion.

That way, if you had to sell the property, you could quickly recoup your investment and even make a profit.

The very worst thing that could happen is that you end up owning a house at a very deep discount.

If that happens, you can hire a realtor to sell it and make more than the interest return on your investment.

Not really a bad thing.

Next... a higher return is very attractive.

You see, I pay my investors much more than what they can earn in a CD.

How much more?

Well, you'll be surprised at what you can earn and why it still makes sense for both of us.

Let's take a moment and look at how banks make money. Most banks borrow money from the Federal Reserve at the federal funds rate, which at the time of this writing is currently 4.5% (https://www.bankrate.com/rates/interest-rates/federal-funds-rate).

They then lend that money to the typical consumer in the form of a mortgage, line of credit, or some type of loan for an average of *10.73%-12.50%* or more.

Credit score	Average loan interest rate
720–850	10.73%-12.50%
690–719	13.50%-15.50%
630–689	17.80%-19.90%
300–629	28.50%-32.00%

* https://www.bankrate.com/loans/personal-loans/average-personal-loan-rates

That's over a 200% return for them! Borrow low and lend it out at whatever rate you want! (By the way, we'll discuss how you can do the same thing later in this book, so keep on reading!)

Furthermore, if you decide to put money in a savings account or CD, they'll use that same money, YOUR money, to lend it to other people. That's right. They'll use the money that you deposit and lend it out to other people. They'll make 10% or more on YOUR money and pay you about 1% interest if anything.

While we're writing this, according to Bankrate.com, "The average five-year jumbo CD rate is 1.24 percent." And by the way, you have at least $100,000 invested for five years to get that 5-year jumbo CD rate. A regular 1-year CD with less than $100,000 gets you an average rate of only 1.47%.

Find current CD rates and recent interest rate trends from Bankrate below. Here are the current average annual percentage yields (APYs) for the week of Feb. 1:

- 1-year CD yield: 1.47% APY
- 5-year CD yield: 1.18% APY
- 1-year jumbo CD yield: 1.55% APY
- 5-year jumbo CD yield 1.24% APY
- Money market account yield: 0.27% APY

The national average rate for one-year and five-year CDs started to increase last February, driven in part by rising Treasury yields and expectations of Federal Reserve rate increases in 2022.

You thought that was bad?

Again, according to Bankrate.com, "The national average interest rate for savings accounts is 0.19 percent."

So, that $100,000 you put in a CD will earn you a whopping $1,240 per year!!! If you decide to put it in a "savings" account instead, you'll earn an incredible $190 a year!

In the meantime, they'll lend your money to someone else and earn $10,000 a year or more… on your money!

They receive the difference, which is referred to as "The Spread." "The Spread" amounts to billions of dollars a month for them. That's why the banks have the big buildings.

Are you ready to be the bank instead?!

If you decide you want to be like the banks, you too can earn a high return regardless of what's happening in the stock market!

That's right!

You can rely on your investment without worrying about the principal fluctuating. When you work with me, the principle remains the same! Keep on reading as I dive more into this later in the book!

Now, you may be wondering, "why would anyone be willing to pay a high rate of return to a private lender like I do?"

Well, it's because the quick availability of funds is more important than paying a lower rate to the bank.

I look at my lenders like silent partners. I give them a high, dependable, and safe return secured well by real estate, and they supply the short-term capital to grow my business. It is a win-win for everybody.

Plus, banks require applications, extra time to close, and extra closing costs, and they have limits on the number of loans they can make to any single company or individual investor.

You see, I can move much faster without these limitations by using private lenders. As a result, I can negotiate more profitable deals while offering sellers a quick and easy sale of their property.

Using private money, I can offer all cash to a motivated seller, helping them out of their financial situation, giving me a great deal with lots of equity, and giving you, my private lender, a great return on your investment safely and secured by real estate!

It's a win-win-win situation!

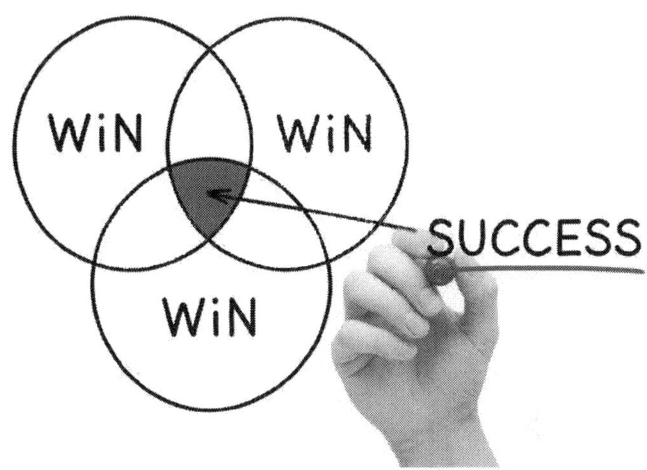

Incidentally, making high-interest loans is nothing new. There are companies in your city doing it right now and have been for over 40 years or more. They're called finance companies or secondary lenders.

It's a multi-billion-dollar industry.

Companies like The Money Store, Coastal Finance, Beneficial Finance, Household Finance, AVCO, and American General are just a few examples.

Their specialty is helping people who want to refinance or purchase a home to live in but can't qualify for a nice low-interest loan.

And before I get off the subject, pull out one of your credit card statements and look at the rate.

Congratulations!

You also are a person like me who is willing to pay a high interest rate for short-term money that's easy to get.

Besides their "special introductory offer," most credit cards charge anywhere between 12% - 28% interest on your balances.

That's right!

Over 20% interest that you have to pay them!! And, of course, the reason you're willing to pay that is that you're placing the availability of funds above the cost of funds every time you use one of those cards.

Like I said, it's a multi-billion-dollar industry.

So, why don't you become the bank?

If you can borrow money at a low rate and safely lend it out at a higher rate, you can make a fortune off the spread.

Now, you're making the spread yourself and not leaving it up to the banks!

Don't you just love it?!

Plus, if you aren't using your own money, you have the best rate of return of all.

It's called infinity.

You see, when you have none of your own money invested, you can't measure the return.

How do you do that?

Well, of course, you borrow it!

For example, I know of one particular private lender who loaned out over a million dollars in one year.

And check this out... he had borrowed all the money to loan out and charged twice what he was paying.

In fact, he used a credit line so he wouldn't have to pay interest while the money wasn't in use. When it was in use, he only had to pay 5%, and he charged 10%!

Using his $1 million line of credit he borrowed from the bank, he made $50,000 in one year – with none of his own money!

Well, I'm sure you have other questions concerning private lending, and while I'll cover everything in a lot more detail later on in this book, let me answer the most common ones right now.

First, let's start with, "Can I use my IRA or 401(k) to make these loans?" And the answer is a resounding YES!

You bet you can. Absolutely.

It's an excellent use for your IRA funds, and what better way to go than tax-deferred or, in the case of a ROTH IRA, tax-free?

If you want to use IRA funds, it must be in a self-directed IRA account.

Now, this is easy to accomplish, and it's only a matter of moving it to an administrator of your choice. If you still need to get one, I've been able to build a relationship with a great company out of Texas. They have thousands and thousands of IRAs, and I think you will find them a pleasure to deal with.

Now don't worry; when you work with them, you don't have to do a rollover with penalties from the IRS. It's merely a transfer from your current administrator to another one.

If you're going to use your IRA to make loans, you'll find this a necessary step because most people have their IRAs housed with a company that will not allow them to make loans or, in fact, do any kind of investments other than what's on THEIR list. We call those multiple-choice IRAs ...but not truly self-directed IRAs.

With a true self-directed IRA, you can do whatever you want with your money, not what someone else insists you do.

Now, if you're using a 401(k), you must be in control or be able to write a check.

Getting your employer to direct the pension plan into private loans will be very difficult. They're usually managed by stock brokers with set guidelines. They'll do what they want, and you won't change their mind.

However, if you have left a job or retired, that 401(k) belongs to you, and by law, your previous employer has to allow you to transfer it to a traditional IRA.

In this case, you'll want to check into transferring it to the company I'll share with you, and then you can start making private loans and truly start self-directing it.

I know of several private lenders that take the money out of their private plan and shift it into their own self-directed IRAs.

You might want to consider the same if it applies to your circumstances and if your company plan doesn't have a history of a high rate of return that you're happy with.

Another question you might ask is, "Does being a private lender constitute selling a security, or will I be pooling funds?"

The answer is yes and no.

Technically, any debt instrument is a security. But it's not a security that you'll need a license for or have to register with the SEC or anything of that nature.

In other words, you will be completely compliant with any and all SEC regulations when you do it properly and the way I discuss in this book.

You will own the whole loan with no other participants. You are in control all the way, which in itself makes this a better investment than any other vehicle I know. Only when loans are pooled does it become a security.

When I find a house, I know what it takes to get the job done.

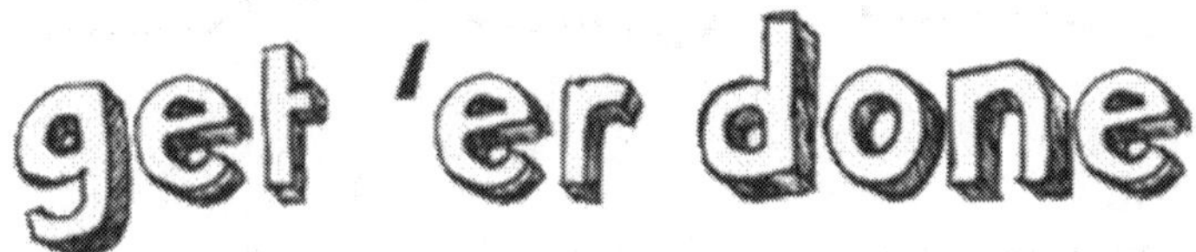

If I need to borrow more than you have available, then I'll have another private lender come to the table. In some cases, I can fund the deals with more than one investor by simply giving one investor a first mortgage or deed of trust and the other a second.

Two separate loans but secured by the same property.

Of course, the second mortgage holder will know it's a second mortgage and be willing to accept the inferior position in exchange for an even higher rate of return than a first deed of trust.

But frankly, it shouldn't matter as long as the total loan-to-value ratio doesn't exceed 75% of the after-repaired value.

For example, if the property's value is $100,000 and I need to borrow $75,000... I can split the loan into a $50,000 first mortgage and a $25,000 second mortgage. Both loans are still well secured because the total loan-to-value ratio doesn't exceed 75%.

The next question is, "Who handles the paperwork?"

Here's what sets my program apart from most other programs and what sets a professional investor apart from someone who's just starting or doesn't really know what they're doing.

So, let me first start by saying that it won't be me, and it won't be you.

You should never write a check directly to me or my company.
Let me say that again...

For your safety and the "professional" investors' safety, you should never write checks directly to someone unless they are an attorney or a qualified professional!

This, of course, leads me to the answer. All real estate closings should be done by a real estate attorney or a title company, or an escrow company.

Your check will be made out directly to the closing agent for the gross amount of the loan. In addition, I will pay all closing costs.

This is standard procedure when you work with me. I follow the same procedures as any commercial bank to ensure a high level of professionalism and security for my private lenders.

When you follow my procedures, it then becomes the Real Estate Attorney's responsibility to receive your funds and ensure that all the documents are in place to secure your investment.

You don't do any paperwork; you simply agree to make the loan and get the money to the Real Estate Attorney when it's time.

A few more quick questions like, "How am I protected against fire loss and making sure the title is clear of liens?"

Answer?

First, I purchase title insurance as part of the closing costs on all purchases to ensure we have a clear and clean deed. It will be issued naming you, the lender, as the insured. This protects you against title defects that could affect your collateral.

Some investors just accept checks from private lenders and "hope" that nothing happens.

My goal is always to operate with a high level of professionalism as well as to ensure the safety and security of the funds I receive from my private lenders. Therefore, I make sure to go above and beyond to make sure that happens.

In addition to title insurance, I purchase fire insurance as part of the closing costs. I want the fire insurance company naming you, the lender, right on the policy, so if the house burns down, you get a check for the full amount of your loan.

When you receive your package after the closing, it will contain the original note and a copy of the deed of trust, which will be recorded at the courthouse. Again, the Real Estate Attorney represents you and makes all this easy for you, and ensures proper execution. A lot of people ask me, "Is this a long-term investment?"

The answer is, well, that's up to you and me.

Most loans are interest only and range from one-year to three-year balloons with all the principal due. However, this can be arranged any way you want it arranged.

It comes down to whatever it takes to meet your investment needs and your investment plan. But, of course, the longer the money stays out at a higher rate of return, the faster it's going to grow.

Another one of the benefits of working with me is that I make interest-only payments. This means that you're earning interest on the entire principal all the time.

Some investors make amortized payments which means you'll get interest and principal payments – similar to a 15-year or 30-year fixed mortgage.

This might sound good since you're getting some of your principal back with your payments, and in reality, if you get a little piece of the principal every month on an amortized loan, that little piece is no longer receiving a higher rate of return.

This means your money does not grow as fast since you have less of it at work every month.

Because of how my program works, most of my private lenders like to keep the money out and collect interest-only payments on a regular basis.
Now, I know that "life and circumstances" happen to all of us. So, while most of my private lenders keep their funds with me, I have built into my program a way you can "cash out" if the need arises.

One more question before we dive into the contents of this book.

"Is making private loans really a safe investment?"

If you apply common sense and don't break the rules that I have in place to protect you, it's as safe as any other high-yield investment and a whole lot safer than most.

In my opinion, it's a lot safer than the stock market.

Think about it.

With stocks, you're betting on

companies you know little about, and the volatility of the market is out of your control. You can do well one year and get wiped out the next.

Every day you're wondering whether you're gaining or losing, and the only choice you get to make is when to buy or when to sell. Now that's risky.

We've had several stock market crashes in the recent past, notably in the year 2000 with the "Y2K" scare, then again in 2008 after the housing bubble, and once again in 2020 due to the COVID shutdown.

I can't tell you how many people came to me and told me that their 401(k) was now their 41(k)! (Just a little stock market humor there... except; unfortunately, many people actually experienced a HUGE loss in their portfolios!)

I don't care how good you are. The fact remains... you don't get to make the rules in the stock market. Your investment is at the mercy of ever-changing circumstances.

Now, compare that to private mortgage loans as a private lender. With mortgage loans, your return is fixed and won't change regardless of whether the market is up, down, or sideways. So, while the stock market spirals downward and other investors are watching their portfolios shrink ... you'll be smiling because today's fickle circumstances didn't affect your money.

Your loans are secured by real estate that you can see, and they aren't going anywhere regardless of what the stock market does. So, you have a large hedge factor to protect yourself if things don't go as planned. Remember, the maximum loan amount is only 75% of the after repaired value.

You get to agree to the rules, not be a slave to someone else's rules.

The term, rates, and conditions are what you and I say they are. There's no guesswork as to what's going to happen. You and I will be building our business relationship that could lead to other lucrative opportunities or joint ventures.

You see, when people like us build wealth together and prosper from each other's efforts... it sometimes even leads to other opportunities.

I don't know of any other investment opportunity that gives the safety, stability, and high return that private lending offers. Has this quick introduction piqued your interest yet?

Are you ready to be the bank yourself and start earning a high rate of return on your investments Safely and Securely?

If so, keep on reading!

And after you've finished reading this book (or even before you finish), if you decide to become my next private lender, just reach out to me, and we'll have a conversation. Then, when we're done, you'll know exactly what to count on and how to move forward.

Remember, the purpose of this book is not to sell or solicit any type of security, fund, or investment product to you. In fact, if you called me out of the blue and said, "Sign me up as your next private lender," I wouldn't do it! I would need to get to know your situation and determine together if this is the right thing for you.

The real purpose of this book is to introduce you to the world of private lending and what that could mean for you and then possibly explore working together down the road.

I invite you to read through this book and then reach out to me so we can discuss what those possible next steps might be if any

By the way, maybe we haven't met yet because you found my book online, or maybe someone gave you this book because they thought it might open your eyes a bit and be beneficial to you.

If that's the case, before I dive into exactly how you can get high rates of return safely and securely, I'd like to tell you a little about myself and how I got into this real estate business.

I'm a firm believer in working with people you know, like, and trust, so hopefully, you can get to know me a little bit through this book, and I'll get to know you when you reach out.

And so, the story begins...

You Can Be The Bank

" I just live by the ABC's - Adventurous. Brave. Creative."

-- The Secret Life Of Walter Mitty

My Secret Life

Hi! My name is Corbin, Todd Corbin. Most people know me as a hardworking, straightforward, nice guy—a mild-mannered man of God and a member of the church band. Of course, all of that is true.

I don't oversell or talk a bunch of fluff. People tell me that I am genuine. I am actually quite turned off by people who talk a great game but don't come through when it all comes down to it. When I say I am going to do something, I do it. I am honest and trustworthy.

That might sound pretty plain to most people.

And I'm okay with that. I have a beautiful wife of almost 30 years at the time of this writing, Liana, who was an elementary school teacher for over two decades. She's now tutoring kids and loves it – all the teaching without the administrative headaches. To most people, we live a simple, plain life, and I'm happy that people know us that way.

Corbin, Todd Corbin

Most people don't see the other Todd Corbin – the international man of mystery, the American spy in Cairo, the Bible smuggler in China, the Indonesian concert "phenom," or even the recipient of an angel sent from God. Sounds fantastic, right? Well, I'll let you be the judge of that.

You see, the mild-mannered Todd Corbin you might know or have heard about is a man driven by his passion for helping people worldwide, enabling him to see and do some incredible things. Things that other people only dream about. Things which you'll learn about in this chapter.

You might even say that I've been on a mission my entire life... well, multiple missions, that is. As of this writing, I've been to 6 of the 7 continents. I have traveled to all 50 states, as well as over 50 countries around the world. I have directed and/or performed in 18 theater productions in the US and Hungary and have done concerts in 15 countries around the world.

I have had my share of adversity, but it has only strengthened me. God has used each difficulty in my life to mold me into the man He wants me to be. I have learned that when trouble comes, I have a few choices. I can run, I can shut down, or I can fight and learn from each trial.

I'll share some of these stories with you in this chapter. How will these amazing stories affect you? That, I can't predict. What I can predict, however, is that they will give you some insight into who I really am and why, if you decide to work with me, you can have some comfort in knowing that you can believe what I say to you; I'm not a quitter, not afraid of adversity; and will do everything in my power to help you in whatever it is you're looking to achieve.

This world runs on stories; I believe everyone has a story – even you. This chapter is my story. As you read it, I hope you get to know me better, get a feel of how I think, and see how I operate. If you like what you read, reach out to me, and let's get to know each other. I'd love to get to know you as well.

Emotional Damage

HOWEVER, before I get to some of those stories, let me start at the beginning...

I was born in a small town in Ohio. My dad was a service manager at a car dealership my grandfather and great-uncle owned. For most of my formative years, my mom was a stay-at-home mom. I also have two brothers (I'm the middle child)—just a good old midwestern family.

When I was around the age of 4, I started picking out songs on the piano. Well, everyone said I must be a "genius" to start so young, so they started me on piano lessons. Unfortunately, we didn't have YouTube back then; otherwise, I might have been an international sensation! Alas, no Justin Bieber fame for me, though.

At A Recital

I did enter competitions for music and speech when I was in high school. They were state and national competitions for an association of Christian schools nationwide. In my senior year in high school, I took 1st in state for piano, 1st in vocal, and 1st in public speaking. That same year, I took 3rd in the nation for piano! The competitions were for Christian high schools, so I didn't gain national fame or fortune. They just helped channel my passion for music.

I love music because it allows me to express my emotions, channel my passion, and bring people together. Regardless of what language, religion, or nationality you are, music unites people. It's a great unifier I could use worldwide to connect with people.

Anyway, I was a pretty normal kid. We always had a lot of laughter and fun in our house. Yes, there were times I got in trouble like any other kid. I fought with my brothers sometimes. Other times, I hung out and played games with them. We were just kids growing up.

Growing up, we went to church regularly, and my father even taught a Sunday school class or two, but he never wanted to be a preacher. In fact, someone once said to him, "Oh, you'd make a good preacher." To which his response was, "That's the last thing I'll ever be." When I was in high school, my dad would say the same thing to me, "You're going to be a preacher someday, Todd." I didn't say anything, but in my mind, I could only think, "It'll be a cold day in hell before that ever happens!" Life's funny that way.

Regardless, in my earlier years, my mom was the more spiritual of my parents. She would take us boys to a summer Christian camp where she would work as a counselor. One year, she finally convinced my dad to go. When he was there, he saw a sign on the wall in the dining hall that said, "Only one life will soon be passed; only what's done for Christ will last." That one line was something he said he could not get out of his mind

It's amazing how just one sentence can change a person's life... and the lives around them. When I was about 12 years old, my grandfather and great-uncle were going to retire and turn over their car dealership to my dad and his cousin. At this time, my dad, recalling that one sentence from that sign on the camp dining hall wall, felt God was calling him to be a pastor. So, he said, "no."

Instead of taking over the dealership, he moved the family from Ohio to Tennessee so he could go to Bible school. Then, when I was 15, he finished Bible school, and we moved to Michigan. There, he became the pastor of a church. It is the only church he ever pastored. He stayed there till he retired. One sentence changed his entire life. It also changed mine.

So basically, I had a happy childhood, that is, until I didn't. Soon after my dad became a pastor, it became a regular occurrence that people in the church would go to my parents, offended by something my younger brother or I had done. They told him, "These are not things that Christian kids should do!"

Apparently, we did a lot of things that Christian kids shouldn't do, so we were constantly in trouble.

Because it was his first church, and he had to deal with all these upset people, he kept telling us, "Don't do this anymore. Don't do that anymore. Don't do this anymore!!"

Of course, I'd argue with him...

Often, he would come home at the end of a day and say, "I think we should stop doing this particular activity (it was always something new that we had always done in the past with no issues, but was now taboo)..."

And I'd say, "What is the reason this time?"

And he'd say, "Because so-and-so in the church..."

And I'd say, "Oh my gosh. When does it stop? When can we just be us?!?"

And then I'd get in trouble.

I'd grown up in church, so it wasn't anything new to always be in church, but I was not used to everybody watching my every move! And apparently, I kept messing everything up!

Finally, one Sunday morning when I was 17, I missed the high school Sunday school class. I was going to have to play the piano for the church service that day, and right before everything started, my best friend came running up to me and said, "You better be glad you weren't in the high school class today!"

And I asked, "Why?"

He responded, "The whole lesson was about you."

I said, "What do you mean it was about me?"

He said that the teacher said, "You're a bad influence on his kids, and he doesn't want you around them."

I said, "How do you know he was talking about me?"

He said, "He named you several times and said, 'I don't care if he is the pastor's son. Todd Corbin's a bad influence on my kids.'"

It devastated me!!! I couldn't even react because it was time for church to start, and I needed to play for the service. So, I just sat at the piano and played for the service, but I was dying inside.

I made it through the entire service and ran to my mom as soon as it was over. I was crying and told her what happened. She just said, "Let's just go home."

And we went home.

When my dad finally came home, I told him what had happened, and he said, "Get in the car. We're going to this guy's house."

I said, "No, I don't want to go to his house."

He said, "No, you get in the car; we're going." So, we went.

When we got there, Dad asked the guy to come outside. I can still see it as if it was yesterday. We were standing outside his house. I was standing behind my dad, and my dad defended me, but I was 17, and all I could think was, "This whole thing is your fault because this never happened until you took this job! And since you've taken this job, I'm not good enough for anybody."

EMOTIONAL DAMAGE!

After that incident, I hated my father for two years. Literally hated him... quietly, though. It was extremely traumatic, especially since I internalized everything.

Fortunately, I have a great relationship with him now though. It took me a while to realize it, but I believe God allowed me to go through that experience because He prepared me for what I've been doing for the past 18 years. Since 2005, I've been ministering to the teenage and young adult kids of missionaries. My experiences as a pastor's kid have given me a platform with these young people that I never would have had had I not gone through those things.

My father never knew that I hated him during those years. In fact, I finally told him just a few years ago. He said, "What??!? Why didn't you tell me?"

I said, "EMOTIONAL DAMAGE!"

No, not really. I said, "I didn't want you to quit because of me. I couldn't handle that kind of guilt. I didn't want you to be angry, so I just kept it in."

He said, "I feel like I was a horrible father."

I said, "Dad, I was 17. That's the way I internalized it at that age."

He responded, "But I feel horrible."

I said, "No, Dad, What Satan meant for evil in my life, God meant for good."

I now look at those experiences I had as a teen as a gift from God. Even though it was painful, it was a gift enabling me to have the ministry I've had for the past 18 years."

That incident at age 17 was only the beginning of many times that I was made a public example during my early adult years. I served in some very legalistic churches and schools and was constantly in trouble.

I'll just be honest. I'm not a conformist. By nature, I'm much more... well, let's say I will be my own person. And it has made me stronger. In addition, it has deepened my faith in God in a strange way.

People have asked me, "How did you not turn against God when all that happened with your dad's church and so on?" And I said, "I don't know. All the times that I got hurt by spiritual men, I never turned it toward God. I guess it was because I could separate them from Him and realize they were not God doing this to me. They are just men."

You might say that perhaps "God just wants me to go through Hell so that I can learn how to handle things properly!" Ha ha ha.

Superstar!

And you know, you can never predict how life will turn out. The best you can do is listen to your heart and work your behind off to achieve what you want.

Sometimes you don't know what you want, though. Coming out of high school, I didn't really know what I wanted to do. Since music had always been a significant part of my life, I decided to major in music, specifically piano, with a speech/theater and Bible double minor. Although I was determined not to conform to anyone's plan or hope for me, I attended the same university where my father attended Bible School and my brother went to university.

Upon graduation from college, I became a high school teacher. I taught music, speech, driver's ed., and theater. During one of those years, someone with whom I had attended college reached out to me. Janet had grown up as a missionary kid in Indonesia and the Philippines. In college, Janet and I sang and performed together.

So, one day, during my third year of teaching, Janet connected with me and said, "I'm going on a mission trip to Indonesia. You want to go? We can be the music."

What she meant was that she and I would be singing Christian music while a pastor and missionary did all the speaking. Having lived in Indonesia for a few decades, the missionary organized everything, and we went from island to island, singing, preaching, and building relationships.

After One Of The Concerts In Indonesia

We went to one city with a population of 100,000. This city was on one of the islands that is now part of New Guinea. Most of those people had never seen a white person before. So, when the news hit that a group of American white people were coming, the people were ecstatic. I remember as the ship we were on was pulling into the port, another ship was leaving. A man ran from one end of his ship to the other, snapping pictures like crazy. These white foreigners were a genuine phenomenon for these people.

When we exited the ship and started going through the city, there was a big banner with our names on it spanning the city's main street. The city's mayor also welcomed us and presented us with gifts. For four nights, we did concerts in that city on a platform at one end of a soccer field. Let me tell you; there was an ocean of people just standing there listening and watching us... the organizers estimated upwards of 25,000 people came each night. That's nearly 1/4 of the entire city!

They wanted to touch us, rub the hair on our arms, get our addresses, and even our autographs. We were celebrities to them. Keep in mind, I had never done anything in missions before, so I was thinking, "Hey, if this is mission work, sign me up!"

On the last night of our time there, Janet and I decided that, during the instrumental intro on one of our songs, we would lean down and try to shake the hands of a few people—big mistake!! Pandemonium broke out as the entire crowd started pushing toward the stage just to have a chance to touch the Americans. They began to pull us off the stage and would have succeeded had the security guards not stepped in.

Each night when the concerts ended, long lines were waiting to get our autographs!! If we had let it, we would have signed papers all night. Eventually, the guards would have to surround us to put us into a couple of jeeps to leave the area. And, without fail, night after night, the people would be screaming and banging on the windows because, to them, we were like the Beetles! It was fantastic! Crazy... and fantastic!

Todd Corbin... Superstar! Not really, but I must admit, I felt like I was.

I was able to impact the lives of literally thousands of people because of music and ministry... or because I was a white American. And hey, maybe the people came because I was white, and they stayed for the music and the message! It was quite the experience to be able to reach out to so many people in just a couple of months!

Adventures In Babysitting... and China

Also, during this time, while I was teaching in Los Angeles, I had gotten connected with an organization in Hong Kong that looked for foreigners to carry Bibles into China. That was the only way people could get a Bible in China unless they were members of the State church.

For years, China had only allowed sales of the

Bible through official channels, so there was always a demand for Bibles – especially in underground churches. These are Chinese churches in the People's Republic of China that had chosen not to follow the state-sanctioned church. Plus, under Chinese law, bringing "harmful" material into the country is illegal if it exceeds the amount for personal use. The Bible is on the "harmful materials list."

While there is no penalty for Westerners caught smuggling Bibles, they confiscate them if found. In these cases, they would give you a receipt and tell you, you can pick them up on your way back out. Even though we would be in no danger bringing in Bibles, it was still a bit unnerving to realize we would be smuggling Bibles into Communist China!!

I believed in the cause of bringing Bibles to the people in the underground church of China, so I organized a group of my high school students to accompany me on a mission of smuggling Bibles. We ended up being a team of 14: myself, another teacher from the school in LA, a young woman, and 11 students.

The Smugglers

Upon arrival in Hong Kong, we were introduced to the guy who would provide us with little pocket-sized Bibles to bring in and who would also travel with us across the border. These Bibles had nothing written on the outside, so you couldn't tell they were Bibles – they just looked like little books.

So, we went to this guy's apartment the day before we would go into China, and he said, "Take anything out of your luggage that you're not going to need to make space for these Bibles." He told us to "be creative" in finding places to hide them. We had a bunch of little snack bags, so we emptied each of their contents, and one Bible would fit in each one. We stuck them in socks, in underwear, anywhere we could. We got creative.

On the day we went in, I wore pants that had a bunch of pockets all over, and I had a Bible in each pocket. One girl had a special slip made to wear under her dress that had 50 pockets in it. She put 50 Bibles in that slip under her dress that day. She was kind of a tiny girl, but she looked a bit fluffy that day.

Our guide said, "It would be best for us to be on the first train of the morning because the border guards would be less awake, making our chances of getting through undetected much better."

Seriously, that's what he said! I'm not kidding you!

He then said, "And when we get to the train station in Hong Kong, everybody's on their own. Do not talk to each other because there are spies all over Hong Kong, and if they hear you talking, they could tell the guards up at the border to watch for us." So, as soon as we got to the train station, we all suddenly became "total strangers."

Well, we were supposed to be all alone until one of the high schoolers came over to me and said, "Corb!" That's what they called me back then. I said, trying not to move my lips, "You're not supposed to be talking to me!" He said, "I lost my passport!!!"

I think I heard a "thud" as my heart hit the ground. The train was about to arrive, and I said, "Oh my gosh!!!" Thinking frantically, I tell him, "Go over there to the... to the thing, and ask if somebody's turned one in and everything!"

You know, the thing, right? Hey, I was lucky I could even think at that point.

And so, he goes over to that thing, like he knew what I meant because he could read my mind or something. Seriously, we were all nerve-racked.

Well anyway, the train came, and I didn't know what to do. I looked at the other teacher, and as the train pulled up, he said, "I'll stay with him!"

The rest of the kids had already started boarding the train to the border, so I also pushed my way on! I mean, there were so many people that you had to shove your way to get on this thing, or you'd miss it.

If it wasn't already enough that I was worrying about the kid who lost his passport, I then noticed that our female chaperone did not make it on the train either. The doors closed right in front of her! Unfortunately, there was nothing I could do except watch her stand there as the train slowly pulled away, leaving a teacher, a high school kid, and a female chaperone behind. The other ten kids and I headed towards the Chinese border.

This was long before cell phones were commonplace, so I had no idea how we would reconnect with them later. I had no idea if this kid was going to find his passport, and I had all these Bibles shoved into my pockets, with no guide and ten kids who I supposedly "didn't know." What an adventure!

Anyway, we got to the Chinese border, heading into Guangzhou. It's in Southern China, and at one time, it was called Canton. Our guide told us earlier, "When you get to the border if you come to the area where the X-ray tables are and you see any of the group having their Bibles taken out, don't go through yet because the guards are alerted." "Stall," he continued, "find something to do."

So, as I came around the corner where the X-ray tables were, I saw three of my students having their Bibles removed...

Right. I'm thinking, "Okay...ummm."

Being the quick thinker I am, I went to the bathroom for a while. You know, you can only stall in the stall for so long, so I eventually came back out. I knew you had to fill out some forms for customs, so I headed over to the table with the forms on it. I kept letting people get in front of me to get theirs. I'm sure everyone thought what a polite person I was...or maybe they thought, "What is the idiot still doing here?"

Anyway, once I got the forms, I pretended to

knock them over and drop them on the ground—anything I could do to stall. I'm sure I looked pretty strange and obvious, and what else was I going to do?

Finally, I sat down somewhere and started filling out the form. I kept glancing over to the customs check, and as I did, I now saw a fourth student getting their Bibles removed.

So, I was sitting there, seeing this happen out of the corner of my eye, but I was sweating bullets and, with my eyes open, praying like there was no tomorrow because I had 80 Bibles in my luggage.

I mentally said, "God, you brought us here. This is the only way these people can get a Bible. I'm asking you somehow to blind the customs agents so they don't see me." I continued, "But I'm going to sit here until I sense you're telling me to go." Since I had no idea what to do, I was waiting for a sign!

As I was sitting there praying and looking around, I happened to notice that there was one place where all the foreigners HAD to get their passports stamped. Just past that, to the left, was an X-ray table. It was logical that you would go to that table because it was the closest, but there was no sign saying you HAD to go to that X-ray table. In addition, there were very few foreigners going through it, so it was easy to be very thorough with everybody.

I then noticed to the right, there were hundreds of Chinese people going through a different line, and I thought, "I wonder if I could get my passport stamped and then be the dumb foreigner that doesn't realize I'm supposed to go through the short line and instead, go to the long line over there with hundreds of Chinese people. Maybe I could slip through unnoticed." Unnoticed?? Seriously?? Think about how you might stick out in a crowd of hundreds of Chinese people, Todd.

I was sitting just wondering, "Should I do that? Should I do that? Should I really do that?" And then I noticed this guard standing there with a gun watching me. AWK!!! And while I was freaking out, thinking about what to do next, another one of my students was having his Bibles taken away!

In a split second, though, his eyes caught mine. Just then, I saw him inconspicuously slide his finger back and forth under his nose to point to those other X-ray tables on the right, and I immediately thought, "Okay, that's my sign. God's telling me that's what I'm supposed to do."

I could feel my heart pounding through my chest

as I got up and got my passport stamped. I immediately turned to the right and was sure that at any second, somebody would yell at the "dumb foreigner" to get over to the line on the left. Surprisingly, nobody said anything, and I arrived at the lines on the right.

There were two rows of X-ray tables and hundreds of Chinese people going through, and two customs agents were standing in the middle, telling everybody to put their luggage on the X-ray tables. One was looking in one direction, and the other was looking in the other direction, so I thought, "Okay, I'll just walk between them, and they won't notice me, right?"

If only things would be so easy...

When I got to them, they turned and started talking to each other. And, of course, here I was, walking right between their noses. And neither one of them said a thing. So, picture this. I'm way taller than any of the people over there. I'm the only person who doesn't have black hair. In fact, I was the only foreigner in the entire area, AND I was the only person walking straight down the center of a sea of Chinese people.

I actually passed eight workers who were telling everybody to put their luggage on the X-ray tables. And no one said a word to me. I walked straight on through and crossed the border into China. God did cause those customs agents to not see me, and all of my 80 Bibles made it through.

And in case you were wondering, the student who had lost his passport found it. Somebody had turned it in, fortunately. He, the other teacher, and the woman chaperone who missed the first train actually got on the very next train and were able to join us just past customs.

Excitement over, right? Yeah, no. That was only the beginning. Now that we were through customs and in China with most of our Bibles, the spy movie-like scenes really began.

So, we went back to our hotel and unpacked everything. We took all of the Bibles and put them into these expandable luggage-type bags that have wheels on them and flatten way down or can be filled up, like waist-high. Regardless, we were able to fill three of those with all these pocket-sized Bibles from everyone who got them through customs.

The guide from Hong Kong looked at me and said, "Okay, Todd, you're going to go with me to deliver the Bibles." I said, "Well, where are we delivering the Bibles to?" He replied, "We're gonna go to a hotel in the city, and you just do what I tell you to do." He said, "Don't ask questions. Don't do anything I don't tell you to do."

At this point, I thought, "Do I need a gun to protect myself? Should I write my last will and testament?" Okay, maybe it wasn't that bad, but still, I was like, "Well, how are we gonna know..." And he cut me off and said, "Don't worry about it. Don't worry about it, and just do what I tell you."

We got to the hotel in the city, and I was walking beside him, lugging these expandable luggage things along, and he whispered to me, "When I tell you, let go of the bag." And all of a sudden, without any warning, he said, "Drop it."

He and I let go of the bags and kept on walking. I was supposed to pretend like nothing happened, but curiosity got the better of me, so I turned around and saw two people walking out the door with those bags. It was like a James Bond switcheroo kind of thing. Crazy!

The guide must have known who those other people were, or they had some signal or something I didn't know. I just know that when he said, "Drop it," I dropped it. And he said, "Just keep walking." Like nothing happened. Yeah, it was a real "Spies Like Us" moment.

After that, our guide was so excited about how many Bibles we had just brought in that he suggested we forget about doing anything else during our time there but instead keep going back and forth across the border carrying countless Bibles.

I said, "No. I don't want to do this the whole time we're here. We want to meet people. We want to be able to talk to them about Jesus. You know, we want to make relationships." Well, he didn't like that answer, so guess what?? He ditched us. He left us there in China and returned to Hong Kong.

Hah! I had just smuggled in Bibles like some spies in a James Bond movie, and now we were being ditched in a foreign country with 11 high school kids and no one in our group speaking the language.

Not quite what we expected when we decided to accept this mission! And since this was our first time doing it, we had no plans, schedule, or idea what to do next! Still, the verse in 2 Chronicles 15:7 says, "Be strong and do not give up, for your work will be rewarded."

So, I told everyone, "Okay. Well, we'll stay here for a week and try to meet people by going to some public places like parks and stuff." Another adventure!

As I said, no one spoke Chinese. We just went out and found public places to hang out. We had a little boombox. We had learned a few songs, and we'd sing these songs and whatever. And people just would come and stand around and listen to us. Some of them wanted to practice their English if they knew any, so we just started talking to people."

Then I decided we were going to go up to Beijing. We did the same thing and met a bunch of people up there, too. After a couple of weeks of singing and sharing, we all went home. Fortunately, no one got arrested. No one got shot. Hah! Lots of great stories, though!

On The Great Wall Of China

Again, what started with music allowed us to spread a message. I know these kids had the adventure of a lifetime, and so did I... well, the first of many for me.

The following year, we did it again. This time, 11 of us went, and we prayed that nobody would have their Bibles removed. Going through customs, all but one of us had to put our luggage on the X-ray tables including me, and no Bibles were found. Everyone was able to get their Bibles in without incident.

No Bus For You!

The year after that, my third year going to China, we had 22 of us. The church we worked with in Hong Kong that supplied the Bibles was confused about how large our group was. So, they didn't bring enough Bibles with them, and on top of that, they were so late getting them to the hotel that we had to scramble in the hotel lobby to secretly pack these pocket-sized Bibles into our luggage before we needed to run to the train station. While I was frantically packing Bibles in my luggage and watching the clock, two of my students came up to me and said, "We didn't get any Bibles. They're all gone."

I told them, "We don't have time. We've got to go."

They said, "But we didn't get any Bibles to bring in."

I said, "I'm sorry. There's nothing we can do. We've got to go."

As we headed to the border, we prayed, "God, please don't let any Bibles be taken away." Once we got to the border, the X-ray tables were not working. Whew! What luck, right?

Since the X-ray tables weren't working, customs decided to randomly choose people to open their luggage and inspect things. Oh no! Out of 22 people, they're for sure going to pick some of us!

Well, they did. They picked 2 people from our group. Can you guess which 2 they pulled out to search? The 2 students who didn't get any Bibles at the hotel. What are the chances? You just can't make this stuff up!

This particular trip was memorable for another reason, though. On this trip, we're all pretty sure we were helped by an angel. There's just no other explanation.

So, what happened?

As usual, we stayed in Guangzhou for a week and then headed to Beijing again to meet more people. I had already arranged for us to stay at the same hotel we stayed in each year in Beijing, but I was a little nervous because our plane would arrive in Beijing at 11:30 at night.

With a group of 22, I thought, "How in the world are we going to get to the hotel? I know there will not be that many taxis for all of us." So, I called the Beijing hotel while we were still in

Guangzhou and said, "Could you please arrange to have a bus there to pick us up and take us to the hotel from the airport?" They said, "Absolutely, we'll take care of it. Not a problem."

Problem solved, right?

So, we flew to Beijing. While we were in the airport in Beijing waiting for our luggage, this guy approached me and asked, "Are you Todd Corbin?"

I said, "Yes."

He said, "You have 22 people?"

I said, "Yes."

He said, "You're staying at the Shiyuan Hotel?"

I said, "Yes."

He said, "I have your bus."

I said, "Okay, we're just gathering our stuff."

We got all our stuff, and it was about an hour's drive from the airport to the hotel. We got there at about one o'clock in the morning and got off the bus. I tried to ask the bus driver, "So how much do I owe you?"

He said something in Chinese and shook his head no. So, I thought, "Oh well, I guess they're just going to include it in the hotel bill." So, I went in, got our rooms, and went to bed.

The front desk called me the following day and said, "Mr. Corbin. Can you please come down here? We need to speak with you." So, I went to the front desk, and they said, "Oh, we are so, so sorry. We could not find a bus for you at the airport. But we're happy you made it here."

What?!?

I said, "No, there was a bus there."

They said, "No, no. We called every bus company in the city, and nobody was available to go at that time of night."

I said, "There was a BUS there."

They said, "Well, okay. Maybe he saw you and wanted to make some money, or he felt sorry for you."

I said, "No. This man, he knew my name. He knew how many people we had. He knew where we were staying, and he wouldn't let me pay him."

Awkward pause.

They just looked at me and said, "We sent no bus."

To this date, nobody knows where that bus came from. No one ever paid that bus driver a single dime or jiao in Chinese currency. I never saw the guy again. Nobody knows where he came from. So, I was like, "Oh my goodness! This is an angel!!!"

After that conversation with the front desk, I was so excited and ran upstairs to gather all the students. I told them the story about the bus driver and said, "You guys, he had to have been an angel!"

One of my students spoke up rather shyly and said, "Umm, I don't think so. He was smoking a cigarette."

And the adventure continues...

That was the final trip I took to smuggle Bibles into China.

We Met Down Under

Well, okay, I didn't meet my wife of 30 years in Australia, but we did meet to go to Australia!

In 1988, I was teaching in Michigan and planning on taking a group of 27 high schoolers on another mission trip to Australia for six weeks. There was only one problem. I couldn't find a female to help. I called the group of kids together since the departure date for the trip was getting close, and I said, "You guys, you better pray because if I don't find a woman, we don't go."

I can't take 27 teenagers by myself and without a female chaperone at that.

Fortunately, one girl raised her hand and said, "I know somebody. She's a teacher in Ohio and would be great with this."

I told them, "Well, you guys contact her. Ask her if she's interested in going and helping out." They did, and they told me she was interested.

I said, "Okay, well then, she needs to come up here. I need to meet her, and I'd like her to meet the group and everything before we go." The kids arranged everything, and before she came up, the kids were showing me pictures of her saying with a grin on their faces and giving me the "Eyebrow Waggle," "Mr. Corbin..." (waggle, waggle)...she's single..."

Cute.

At the time, I had a girlfriend, so I wasn't interested in any kind of romantic relationship, but I did like working with Liana. We made a terrific leadership team. In fact, it was actually years later before we would get into any relationship. We led the trip to Australia that first year and then to New York City the following year. Then it was a few years later, when both of us were almost engaged to someone else, that our paths crossed again, and 10 months later, we led another missionary trip together to Ukraine.

Both of our "almost engaged" relationships had ended at the time of this third trip, so on the last day of the third trip, I asked if I could take her out; two months later, I asked her to marry me. We've been happily married since August of 1993.

Together 30 Years And Counting...

Taking Care of Business

When we got married, Liana left her teaching job and went on mission trips with me. We did mission trips all over Eastern Europe, and at least one of those trips each year ended up being in Hungary.

It was not by our design; it just turned out that way – all God's design. But anyway, through that, Liana and I began to form a good connection with the Hungarian people. Hungary had the most positive response to the gospel. And yet, we had our smallest staff there. So, we said, "Maybe we should consider moving here."

We went to Hungary for 10 months in the fall of 1996 to see if this was a good fit. Our oldest son was only a year old at the time. The first 6 months in Hungary were quite a struggle, but after the 10 months ended, we returned to the United States and prayed about it for about a year. During this time, our second son was born. Then, in the fall of 1998, we decided to move to Hungary for the long term.

We received people on missionary trips instead of going on them ourselves during our time there. In addition, there was a huge interest in English. So, we would do these English camps. They'd be like a week-long camp where the Hungarian people would come, and they'd live at the camp for a week. We'd have a team of Americans come over, and it was all about building relationships with them.

We'd help them learn how to speak conversational English, but at the same time, we were also teaching them about Jesus. It was a very non-pressured, very natural relationship-type thing, and it was very successful.

Outdoor Concert In Budapest

All of the Hungarians who attended our camps, no matter what they believed in, knew that they would be learning about Jesus while there. Many would say, "You know what, I'm not that interested in the Jesus stuff, but I love coming here because I know I can be myself here."

So yeah, the big thing was we just loved them, and many of them learned to speak English pretty well through those camps. It wasn't all rainbows and unicorns during that time, though.

In 1998, before moving to Hungary to stay, Dylan, our youngest, was six months old when he contracted spinal meningitis. He had a stroke during that illness and nearly died. Actually, the day we were going to put our house up for sale to move to Hungary was the day Dylan went to the hospital.

He was in the hospital for two weeks. After that, they said, "He's okay now, but you need to know that something could show up later." And it did in Hungary when he was three.

Through a series of events, when he was three, we had to take Dylan to an American speech pathologist in Vienna to find out what was wrong with him. She told us that Dylan was severely delayed in speech and his comprehension of speech and that we needed to get him out of Hungary, away from two languages, and get him into intense therapy.

What we had thought would be just a year of therapy ended up being two and a half years.

I lived between Hungary and the United States during those two and a half years. We owned a house in Hungary, and I had become the country director for our agency, so I had to keep things running. I would go anywhere from four to six weeks at a time and live in Hungary while the family stayed in Michigan, living in my parent's basement so Dylan could have therapy.

Those were some difficult times for our family. I was living and working in two countries while doing my best to take care of my family, and Liana was left to handle two very active boys alone, one of whom had intense needs.

Well, anyway, sometimes you find yourself in a situation that's not ideal. I've learned that giving up is not an option. Finding a solution, working hard, and getting through it is what's important. Fulfilling your commitments, staying in integrity, and doing what needs to be done is critical to succeed in business, life, or anything else. Basically, you've got to stay focused and take care of business!

An American Spy In Cairo

After those 2½ years, Liana and the kids moved back to Hungary to resume our mission. At one point in time, Liana and I just needed a break.

We had two little kids then and just wanted to get away for a bit. Fortunately, you could get some pretty cheap tickets to a lot of countries that were not too far away. So, we went to a travel agency and found a tour headed to Cairo, Egypt. We decided to join up with them.

It was a group of Hungarians going to Cairo for vacation. We didn't know anybody in the group. However, we learned that some friends of ours who had been living in Budapest and were moving to Hong Kong would be having a stopover in Cairo for a few days to be with some friends of theirs. As we all talked about it, we realized that we would be in Cairo at the same time they were. So, we planned to meet up in Cairo and have a meal together.

We were able to leave our 2 boys with a couple of our team members to babysit them at our house while Liana and I were gone.

Once in Cairo, we were with this tour group, but we decided we wanted to stay at a five-star hotel because the prices were so reasonable. So, we found one while everyone else stayed at three-star and four-star hotels.

Our Hungarian tour guide brought us to the hotel, and when we checked in, they realized that even though we're Americans, we live in Hungary because we had to fill out a form that asked us, "Where do we live," and all that stuff. And we were speaking Hungarian with our tour guide in front of everyone at the front desk.

The next day, we were going to go see the pyramids and started down the road in the van with our tour guide and another couple. It was then I realized that I had forgotten my wallet in the hotel room. Turning to the guide, I asked, "Do you think it'll be okay in the room?" The guide said, "No. We got to go back. You go pick that up."

Well, whenever you leave the hotel, you're supposed to leave your key at the front desk. And so, when we got back to the hotel, I asked for my key. I went to my room, got my wallet, and returned to the front desk. As I gave them my key and was about to leave again, they said, "Oh, while you were out, The American Embassy called for you."

I said, "What?!?"

They said, "Yeah, the American embassy called for you. Here's the number. You're supposed to call this guy."

Who and how in the world would they even know I'm here?

So, I called the number, and a guy answered the phone. Turns out that he's the friend of the couple we knew from Budapest, and he worked for the American Embassy. He does a lot of those secret meetings inside the big bubble in the embassy where nobody can hear what's being discussed. He was calling to tell us the address to his house because we were going to have dinner at their house, along with the other couple.

Oh! That makes sense.

The next day rolled around, and we were in our room. Suddenly, these three guys in suits knocked at the door. I opened the door, and they said, "We need to clean your room."

I said, "Okay..." and got

our stuff, went down, and sat by the pool.

While I was sitting at the pool, I started thinking, "Okay, wait a minute. Something's not right. Three men in suits are going up there to clean the room, and they didn't have a cart or anything?? No way."

So, I went back up there, put my key in the door, and went in.

It had only been about 5 minutes. As I proceeded to walk in, the 3 men came out and said, "We're finished," and they left.

Later that night, at dinner, we were at that American Embassy guy's house, and he had all kinds of stories about the government and how they were spying on everything. He talked about how they bugged his house, listened in on his phone calls, and all kinds of stuff like that.

And then I told him what happened with the "cleaning" guys, and he said, "Oh, 100% they were certain you were spies."

I said, "Really?!? Why?"

He said, "Think about it. You show up with this Hungarian group, a very obscure language, and they hear you speaking Hungarian to the guide. But you're Americans, and someone from the American embassy calls." He said, "Without a doubt. They thought you were American spies." He went on, "I'm sure they planted bugs in your room."

Then he said, "Our house is bugged. They're listening now."

Jokingly, I asked, "Which government?"

Without missing a beat, he said, "Both."

I know, I know. I've had a pretty dull life, right?

Miracles Occur

Back in Hungary, we had worked with the church there almost since its beginning. After nearly 10 years there, we finally felt like the church was becoming too dependent on our team. So, the decision was made that it was time for us to pull out. When we did pull out, it was painful because we were very involved in the church.

Unfortunately, people usually look for someone to blame when they get hurt. So, a rumor started saying that I was mad at the church pastor and that I had convinced the team to leave. People said it was my fault for this or that and that I wanted to hurt the church. None of this was true, though. I moved to Hungary to serve in the church! I didn't want to see it damaged! I wanted to see it stand on its own two feet and continue to grow!

For a while, it was, "Todd this and Todd that." It was as if I was that teenage pastor's kid all over again, being blamed for everything and being a bad influence on people. All of it pushed me into a depression. In addition, I started having panic attacks. Finally, in 2007, I was officially diagnosed with severe depression and anxiety. I was sizzled again! Literally, this time!

It came to the point that the leadership of the agency I was working with said, "We need you to leave, or we're going to lose you completely." The idea was to go back to the States for a year to have a sabbatical, get healthy, and then move back to Hungary.

While there were some challenging times during our stay in Hungary, I know God had put us there. The most important thing was that we were trying to improve people's lives. Whether it was helping them get to know Jesus or just helping them learn English, we had a positive impact while we were there.

As I mentioned earlier, things don't always happen as you expect them to. From being blamed as a bad influence as a child to having to live in two countries to take care of my family and my mission, and now, to have the struggles of the church blamed on me, I've always searched for solutions.

I don't oversell or talk a bunch of fluff. People say I am genuine, honest, and trustworthy. I am turned off by people who overpromise and under-deliver. I know when I say I will do something, I do it. I will do all I can to move mountains to come through on my promises.

That said, sometimes you need some help, like the angelic bus driver in China or a cute-looking school teacher from Ohio. And when you believe that what you're doing is right, that you're helping people live a better life, and you're focused on taking the actions to make it happen, miracles occur.

I did everything I could in Hungary until I physically couldn't, and then in 2007, upon the counsel of my superiors, my family and I left and moved back to the United States. That same year, Liana and I were invited to a party at the mission agency we served. At the party, I sat beside this guy who didn't know me at all. For some reason, he started talking about this new position that was opening up in the home office, and that was the start of a conversation that would, once again, change my life.

He told me they were looking for someone with a youth pastor's heart who would start tracking with their college missionary kids. He then starts describing what kind of guy this has to be, his strengths, passions, and all. And wouldn't you know it, every single thing he said described me to a T! Not only that, my experience growing up as a pastor's son and all the missionary trips I've been on made me uniquely qualified for the position.

It was the weirdest thing ever because the guy didn't know me, and he described me perfectly. Like the bus driver in China, this guy seemed to know everything he needed to talk to me about concerning the kind of person they were looking for to fill this position!! I got that job, and like a miracle, this heavy weight was lifted off my shoulders. With the new position, Liana and I decided to stay in the United States and not return to Hungary. It was a new beginning for us!

Liana started teaching again and did so until 2022 when she began tutoring instead. This is what she currently does, and she loves it! All of the education without the administration and bureaucracy.

Who Dun It?

I will wrap things up in a bit, and I want to share one more story with you. Hopefully, you've been able to get a glimpse inside of me and see what makes me tick, tick, tick...

Just kidding. That was a little foreshadowing, and this story is about the bombing in Beirut in 2020. Hey, I didn't do it! Although I was almost stuck there when that happened!

If you don't know about it, according to Wikipedia, "On 4 August 2020, a large amount of ammonium nitrate stored at the Port of Beirut in the capital city of Lebanon exploded, causing at least 218 deaths, 7,000 injuries, and US$15 billion in property damage, as well as leaving an estimated 300,000 people homeless... The blast was so powerful that it physically shook the whole country of Lebanon. It was felt in

Turkey, Syria, Palestine, Jordan, Israel, and parts of Europe, and was heard in Cyprus, more than 240 km (150 mi) away."

In my current line of work, I'm always helping missionary kids. One of the agencies I helped had ministries in many different places, and they were going to lead a team of Americans to Beirut to do an English camp.

I've done lots and lots of English camps, and I was available to help. This was during COVID-19, so many countries were closed, but Lebanon was open. So, I told the powers that be, "Sure, I can go. I can't go anywhere else right now, so why not?"

So, we got together a small team of about ten of us and headed to Beirut, Lebanon.

During our time there, we did an English camp on the side of a mountain overlooking Beirut. My group met outside every day in this little gazebo, and one day, my translator said, "Do you hear that sound above us?"

And I said, "What sound?"

He said, "Can you hear me now?" Oh, wait, wrong commercial... He actually said, "The jets."

And I said, "Oh yeah."

"Do you know who that is," he asked?

I said, "No."

He answered, "Israel."

Okay, that made me nervous. Afraid of what the answer might be, I sheepishly asked, "Why?"

He said, "Because there was some incident where Israel did something to Syria, and now Hezbollah, which is right there in Beirut, was retaliating. And now Israel's trying to do something against Hezbollah."

A bit after that, two military helicopters flew right past the mountain we were on, and I asked, "Is that them too?

He said, "Yes, it is."

And as you can imagine, that was quite unsettling, but nothing happened.

We heard fighter jets flying over top of us for the next few days. More military helicopters flew right past our site as well.

Then, the camp ended. All the Americans headed back to the US, but I stayed for a couple more days. Well, it turns out that the day after I flew out of Beirut, there was a massive explosion that looked like a nuclear catastrophe!

August 4, 2020, Explosion in Beirut

Believe me, I didn't do it! I had already left by then! Like my teenage years and my time in Hungary, though, I wouldn't be surprised if someone blamed it on me. Hah! I'd just have to figure out a way to deal with it like everything else.

So, if I didn't do it, who did it? It was the worker with the door in the warehouse... or was it?

While the official story is that a fire was caused by some workers welding a door, which then caused the explosion, I still wonder, and I'm only speculating if maybe it was Israel that did it? All the things leading up to it... you know, they're flying over, they're upset with Hezbollah, Hezbollah retaliates for Syria, and here was this ship sitting in the port that had all of this ammonium nitrate or whatever, and it suddenly explodes. I guess we'll never know.

So anyway, had I left one day later, I would not have gotten out of Lebanon.

Where I stayed did have damage. I don't think we would have been killed, but some of the people we met at the camp had family members who were killed in that explosion.

Again, someone was watching over me, allowing me to complete my missionary trip and keeping me safe. When I think back on how differently things could have turned out, I feel so blessed that I'm where I am today.

The Journey Continues

My whole life has been a mission to use my experiences to help people and share a message with people all over the world. I've been able to travel to over 50 countries on 6 continents and tell people about how they could have a relationship with Jesus.

Through English camps, I've been able to teach people how to speak English, but it's been more about building relationships with them and introducing them to who Jesus Christ is and how he wants to have a relationship with them.

Through the concerts, it's been the same thing. Sometimes, we weren't always able to build relationships with everyone depending on how many concerts we had to do and how fast we moved to another place, but a lot of times we would stay with families and get to know them that way.

Liana And I In Front Of A Sign Advertising Our Concert In Ukraine

I have a passion for getting to know and help people. Probably partly because of my issues as a pastor's kid and partly just because of how I am wired. I have especially been drawn toward the ones that don't fit into the mold that everyone expects them to.

When I was a teacher, the students who really captured my heart were often the ones that all the rest of the teachers decided were hopeless. Maybe part of it is that I just love a challenge, but I also love seeing if there are paths through the walls these people have frequently built up around themselves for protection.

As I began ministering to the teenage and young adult kids of missionaries, quite a few of them had also built-up walls of protection all around them. Their trust level in people was very low, and understandably so, because of a very mobile life during their formative years. They always felt like the outsider, and no one ever stuck around. I love being able to pour into these young people to let them know how much they matter to God and to the world around them.

God has given me the ability to empathize with people who are hurting. If I can come alongside them and let them know they matter, that they are not alone, and then find tangible ways to help them, I am all over that. I love having conversations that matter.

I have learned that in American culture, you must take things very slowly to go to deeper levels. So, whenever I can find those rare Americans who, like me, enjoy talking about more profound things, I jump at the opportunity to sit down with them and learn about their lives, what makes them tick, etc. I am a very relational person, so going beyond the superficial, surface things with others is my jam.

As I age, the realization starts to hit me that you can't keep up the pace you have for so many years and that I won't be able to invest in these young people like I have been for the past 18 years. That was a bit of a sad realization. However, once I got introduced to the private lending program and the way we invest in real estate, I began to see how this could be another way I could continue to help missionary families for many years to come, even when I'm not physically capable of investing in them the way I have been all these years. That's why I started Integrity Investment Solutions.

Of all the kinds of investing my wife and I have ever done; real estate is the one investment that has never disappointed me. We have always managed to buy low and sell high. We have watched our properties steadily grow in value over the years. Real estate is not a fad; it is here to stay, and people always need a place to live. So, the demand will always be there.

Yes, sometimes you have to pivot because of what might be happening in the world at certain times, but that is the beauty of real estate: you can shift your strategies and still be profitable in multiple ways. And trust me, I know a thing or two about pivoting! There is way more security in real estate than pretty much anything else out there.

Because I am passionate about helping people, especially those who are hurting, real estate is a very tangible and sizable way to help people. When 80% of the population can no longer qualify for a mortgage, our program can help these people get into a home they love while repairing their credit and getting them to a place where they CAN qualify for a mortgage.

On top of that, we love being able to help homeowners who are hurting because they are facing foreclosure or perhaps have inherited a property they don't want to have to keep up. We provide solutions for these people. The whole time we are helping all these people, we are also helping people who become our private lenders by giving them a high rate of return that is fixed and secured by real estate. It is a win-win for everyone all the way around. How cool is that?

So, let's dive deeper into this real estate thing and, of course, the power of Private Lending. I will talk about my private lending program throughout the rest of this book, and I hope this chapter gave you an idea of who I am and what drives me. If you decide you want to work with me, I want to get to know you and your family better as well.

While my life has been one exciting adventure after the next, I'm ready for the next journey in my life... one that will possibly include you and, of course, real estate.

Without further ado, let's dive into the meat of this book!

"How many millionaires do you know who have become wealthy by investing in savings accounts? I rest my case."

-- Robert G. Allen

What Is Private Money And Who Are Private Lenders?

You've probably already heard me mention the terms private money and private lender several times already in this book's introduction. Just to be clear, I want to take some time to properly define these terms so that we're all on the same page. Let's begin with private money.

What Is Private Money

So, what is private money? Well, it's not public money, right?! Wasn't that obvious?

Seriously though, private money is a loan or equity contribution that is not institutional money or money that comes from some kind of commercial business like a bank, credit union, or savings and loan. Basically, it's money from a private organization or individual like yourself.

The term "private money" itself refers to loans made between individuals, i.e., it's "private" between two parties.

So, when you get a "private money" loan, it's typically from a friend, a business contact, or an individual you've built a relationship with.

I'll dive deeper into where you can get private money for a loan, and for now, here's a short list of places that you can look into:

- Checking and Savings Accounts
- Certificates of Deposit
- Money Market Accounts
- Investment Capital
- IRA and Retirement Accounts like a 401(k)
- Home Equity Lines
- Portfolio Loans
- Cash Value Insurance Policies
- Credit Cards

In addition, private money is money that is **liquid** to you or accessible to you to direct wherever and however you decide you want to use it.

Once you identify a source of money that you can personally access, it's a matter of deciding what you want to do with it.

For example, if you've got a $100 bill in your pocket and you want to lend it to your friend Joe, that's private money. You're lending your "private money" to someone else.

Pretty simple and straightforward, right?

Great!!

Let's move on to private lenders then...

Who Are Private Lenders

Well, first, a private lender is an individual just like you, just like me, who loans their money from their investment capital or their retirement account. It's a one-on-one transaction with no broker involved.

And when I say retirement accounts, I'm talking about private lenders using self-directed IRAs in order to loan money out to us real estate investors.

Now, it will be very, very important... and I'll get into this later... it will be very important for you to establish a relationship with a self-directed IRA account representative.

Of course, when you work with me, I'll hook you up with my account rep, who understands how everything works and will walk you through everything step-by-step.

For the sake of simplicity, just know that a private lender is not a bank, not an institution, not a mortgage company... it's an individual that's going to loan money to an investor from either their investment capital or their retirement account.

So again, I'm not talking banks, I'm not talking institutions, and here's another big writ'er downer, and that is... I'm not talking about joint venturing with other people.

A joint venture is when two or more people get together, everyone is responsible for doing something as part of a whole project, and in the end, everyone splits the profit. Equal pay for equal work.

So, I'm not talking about joint venturing here.

A private lender will act in the same capacity as a bank. They are the lender, not a partner.

When a bank lends you the money to buy a house, they're not your partner and won't tell you what color to paint your home, which faucets to put in or change, or what carpet to put in. They're not your partner. They're just a lender.

My private lenders will get the same security and protection as a bank, and they'll act in the same capacity as a bank. In other words, they're a lender... a private lender.

Like the bank, my private lenders will get a promissory note.

In addition, they'll get a mortgage, or in some states, it's a deed of trust, but they're not going to do the rehab, fix up the property, sell, or anything like that.

And just like a bank, they're going to get a high rate of return that's collateralized by an asset worth more than what you lent out. This keeps your investment safe and secure.

A Typical Private Lender

A typical private lender I work with is a friend, a family member, a neighbor, or even a co-worker.

They might be a doctor, dentist, chiropractor, or whatever it is that they do!

They could just be a guy or gal I met while working out at the gym or someone on a rec league I play on.

As a side note, I know someone who runs a group called "Co-Ed Recreational 'only bad players' Basketball." They meet weekly to play some hoops at the local park or indoor rec center during the winter. And from what I hear, most of them are definitely pretty bad! Regardless, they can play horribly and still be a private lender! And hey, I digress...

For further clarification, a typical private lender could be...

- Someone from church that you've known for years.
- Someone retiring or already retired that's looking to grow their cash flow for the rest of their lives.
- A successful business person looking to get higher returns.
- A fellow parent at the PTA.

A typical private money lender (or simply private lender) is Uncle Joe, who just retired from his job and has money in a 401(k) doing nothing; the neighbor down the street who just sold his house and now has some extra cash from the sale and nowhere to put it.

It might be Suzy at the local Rotary club (a service organization), who you've been doing volunteer work with for the past three years and who has a CD that's maturing soon. A CD that she wants to put with someone that can give her a higher return.

An investor named George found out accidentally that, literally, anyone could become a private lender - even a tenant. A few years back, George was looking for private money. He was a landlord and held about ten rental properties, and he needed some private money if he was going to purchase any more.

If you become a landlord and start accumulating properties, you too may find out that banks stop lending to you after you own a certain number of properties. It doesn't matter if you have a positive cash flow on all your properties or not.

Using their calculations, after a certain point, they consider you high risk and stop lending to you. By the way, that usually happens after you've purchased between 5 - 10 properties.

Back to the story. So, it was the beginning of the month, and that was when George usually went to his properties to collect the monthly rent checks.

George lives within 30 minutes of all his properties and manages them himself. So, he goes to all his properties and collects the rents himself each and every month.

While it's not for everyone, George enjoys being a landlord. Collecting the monthly rent allows him to talk to his tenants and check up on his properties.

Well, one of his renters was this little old lady that had been renting from him for almost ten years. She was living in one of his 3 bedroom, 1 bath homes in a low rent area, paying him $600 per month.

When he went to collect the rent, he asked her how she was doing. She said she was fine and had just gotten back from the bank to get more checks just in time for the monthly rent. Then, she asked him how he was doing.

And wouldn't you know it? Since she brought up the topic of banks, he was telling her how his bank wouldn't lend him any more money! So she asked him, "Isn't that what banks do?"

"Ha Ha, Right!?!" he said.

He told her how they told him he was a high risk even though all his properties were rented out to great tenants like her and all his payments were on time.

He said that he would have to start looking for private lenders or people he could borrow money from and pay them a high rate of return instead of a bank.

Now, he wasn't telling his tenant, let's call her Delores, about it so she would lend him some money. He was just having some small talk with her and kind of venting his frustrations with his bank.

Delores started asking him to tell her more about this paying people a high rate of return thing. Not thinking anything of it, he started telling her about private lending.

He told her how he could pay people a good return safely and securely, collateralized by real estate and so on. He was just having a conversation and told her what was on his mind.

Next thing you know, Delores tells George that she's got $500,000 sitting around doing nothing and that she could lend it to him as a private lender.

George was floored!!

"What?" he exclaimed.

After all, Delores was his tenant, renting a house from him for $600 per month.

As far as he knew, she was retired and didn't work anywhere.

How does she have $500,000 to invest with him?

It turns out that Delores was a widow. Of course, George knew this as she had been with him for 10 years.

What he didn't know was that when her husband passed away, she received a substantial life insurance payment.

Since she was widowed and at the time retiring, she didn't want to deal with owning her own home, so she decided to just downsize and rent a house close to her kids. She never needed the large insurance payout; it was just sitting in a bank, earning her about 1% a year in interest.

She just wanted it somewhere safe and secure and didn't invest it in a volatile stock market or some crazy investment, so it just sat there in case she needed it.

Hearing George talk about a safe and secure investment and knowing him for 10 years, she felt comfortable enough to work with him.

George, on the other hand, was, again, floored!

He would never have imagined that his retired tenant of 10 years would have those kinds of funds available to work with him.

Of course, he didn't refuse.

He would be able to go out and purchase more homes, and Delores would be able to dramatically increase her retirement funds safely and securely. It was a huge win-win for both people!

Fortunately, Delores didn't need that extra money, and you know what? After a couple of years, she bought herself a fancy new car she would never have considered purchasing before. It made getting around to her kids and grandkids much easier.

The moral of the story is that you never judge a book by its cover!

Never assume whether someone has money or not. Never assume if someone wants to work with you or not!

Let them decide for themselves if it makes sense for them to work with you!

Of course, the key with George and Delores – and with all my private lenders – is building a relationship and getting to know, like, and trust each other.

The Bottom Line

A typical private lender can literally be anyone that I can build a relationship with and is potentially interested in earning more money on their money. My buddy Jay even had two minors invest their money with him. I'll get more into that story later in the book.

Here's the bottom line.

A Private Money Lender is someone who has access to money that they are willing to lend to someone with the expectation that they will receive some kind of return on that investment.

A Private Money Lender is NOT a professional lender, brokerage, or bank.

That means that if you are not already a lender, broker, or banker, you, and most people out there, can be a private lender...

You Can Be The Bank

"Risk comes from not knowing what you are doing."

-- Warren Buffet

Is Private Lending Safe?

Great question, right? After all, the title of this book is How To Get High Rates Of Return Safely And Securely. So, I'm pretty sure you can guess the answer, correct?

If you haven't, then of course, the answer is a resounding "YES!"... when done properly, that is!

Remember, when done properly and working with the right investor, this is the exact same process that thousands of banks, credit unions, and multi-billion-dollar hedge funds use.

And, of course, they've figured out the absolute best way to protect their own money. And since we're using their same strategies, you, as a private lender, will simply become the bank or credit union, and your money will earn high rates of return safely and securely!

If it's not done properly, well then, of course, you're opening yourself up to all kinds of risks.

Later on in this book, I'll show you the exact steps you need to make sure this happens to ensure your money is safe and secure.

For now, let's discuss some myths, misconceptions, pitfalls, and fears about private money and private lending.

Myths And Misconceptions

A myth that I hear from people all the time is:

Private Lending Is Only For Professionals

Only banks, credit unions, or those quick cash or payday loan places can lend people money, right?

Of course, that's not true.

Anyone can lend anyone else money. People borrow money all the time.

Car dealerships have car loans. Even retail stores like Walmart and Best Buy will finance purchases. You can get cash advances from credit cards. All those are "above board" legal loans.

Then you have Susie borrowing money from her aunt for college or Joe borrowing money from his best bud Clyde for a car repair. Those are usually undocumented, word of mouth, and unsecured loans. Nothing prevents anyone from doing so.

There are specific legal and SEC regulations you must follow if you're going to borrow on a "commercial" level or if you intend to "pool" funds.

No! Not that pool.

Pooling funds means that if you're going to put money from a lot of investors together to make one big purchase, you have to make sure you follow specific guidelines.

Personal loans between friends, family, and acquaintances are not really regulated. And everything you'll learn in this book is in full compliance with any rules, regulations, and laws.

This means that you don't have to be a professional money lender, bank, or institution to lend money and get high rates of return safely and securely. You be you!

Another big myth about private money lending is:

You Have To Be Rich If You Want To Lend Money

Only the rich get richer right?

Again, that's a big myth that I want to dispel. Depending upon the situation, you may only need $25,000 - $50,000 to get started as a private lender. Sometimes even less. I've worked with private lenders for as little as $10,000 before.

Later on, in this book, I'm going to go through an entire list of resources where you might even find money that you've got or can get in order to be a private lender. There's even a method called "arbitrage," which is perfectly legal, where you can get an infinite rate of return because it's not your money!

What does that mean? It means you're borrowing money to lend it at a higher rate. Since it's not your money, to begin with, you're basically getting free money!

Want free money? Then keep on reading, and you'll find out how to do this!

Let's move on to a third misconception before we dive into those resources, though.

Foreclosure Is The Worst Thing That Can Happen When Private Lending

This is the third misconception that many people have. They think that if something happens and you have to foreclose on the property, that could be one of the worst things that can ever happen. And they're worried that they'll lose all their money!

Just to review (and again, I'll go into a lot more detail on how this all works later in the book), when done properly, your money will be secured and collateralized with a property where I've borrowed at most 75% of the after repaired value.

If something happens like I get hit by a bus crossing the street (and in no way, shape, or form do I ever want that to happen!), then you will have a claim on the property that I'm working on.

To redeem that claim, you'll have to initiate the

foreclosure process, which is available in every state.

While it is different in every state, the good news is that it's pretty straightforward and easy to do in many states, provided you have the right paperwork.

Fortunately for you, I'm going to make sure you have the right paperwork. And once it's done, you'll be the owner of the property.

This, too, is a good thing for you because I've only borrowed up to 75% of the after repaired value. This means that once it's fully repaired, you'll own an asset that is worth a lot more than what you've already invested.

The median home price in the US is about $375,000. So if we took the median home price, I would only borrow up to $281,250. That would mean that there's an EXTRA $93,750 in equity that would be yours once it's all fixed up!

This also means that instead of making only a 5% - 10% return on your money, you could be making 20% - 30% or more!

It sounds counterintuitive that having to foreclose on a property could be a good thing instead of the worst possible thing. And while it would take some work, and it may not be ideal (especially for me since I got hit by a bus), it's not so bad for you to make a lot more money when all is said and done!

Common Fears about Private Lending

Let's move on from myths and misconceptions to just some fears you might have as a private lender.

Are There Any Risks With Private Lending?

Let me quote one of my coaches and mentors to answer that question. He broke it down nice and simple by saying, "No Risk, No Goodies!"

As much as it may seem so, there's risk in any kind of investment, even if it's a savings account. Why do you think most, if not all, banks are FDIC insured up to $250,000?

You think your money is safe in a savings or checking account. Did you know that since 2009, there have been 511 bank failures? 511 times, banks have failed and closed.

Fortunately for those bank customers, most of them were FDIC insured and got most, if not all, of their money back. And again, everywhere you put your money, there will be some measure of risk. You just have to decide how much risk you're willing to take and, sometimes more importantly, with whom.

So, yes. There are risks with private lending. AND by following a proven system and duplicating what large banks and institutions have done, my team and I have reduced that risk as much as possible.

You should never trust anyone who says that any investment is 100% guaranteed. I've had 100% guaranteed investments on which I lost a lot of money before.

While I'm a big proponent of the handshake when doing deals, I have also learned to make everything official with contracts and paperwork. And unfortunately, even then, things can go wrong.

I'm not saying this to scare anyone. I'm just addressing a question and being 100% honest about it.

Every investment contains some kind of risk. The trick is to reduce the amount of risk as much as possible.

So, is there risk? Yes.

Can you reduce the risk to make it safe and secure? Yes, depending upon your definition of safe and secure.

Remember your money in a bank? Safe and secure, right? Seriously, how many banks go out of business? (511 since 2009 and many more before that if you didn't already know).

What if the bank was hacked? Would you still get your money?

Again, most people would say, well, yes, it's FDIC secured. But remember, FDIC security is only up to $250,000. What if you had more than $250,000 in the bank?

Well, then the bank would be liable, right? Maybe. You hope.

Again, my point is that simply having your money in a bank doesn't mean it's 100% safe and secure, either.

It does mean that you've reduced the risk as much as possible. And that's what I've done with my private lenders as well.

The next common fear that people have is:
Will I Get My Money Back?

Many factors go into if you get your money back.

One of them is making sure you work with the right people, and another is using the right paperwork.

Again, I'll dive into this later on in the book, and to secure their money, I provide all my private lenders a mortgage on a property that would fully collateralize their money with real estate. This means that their money is backed or secured by real estate. This is the exact same thing that a bank or credit union would do.

Of course, that's only part of the process. A lot of analysis and work is done upfront to ensure I'm getting a great property with great returns for myself and my investors. All this adds to reducing your risk and securing your funds. Make sure you work with someone with a team of people in place that's following a process and/or system and not just shooting off the hip.

When you work with the right people and follow the right process, your money is safe and secure, and yes, barring some unforeseen disaster, you will get your money back – even if the house burns down! I'll tell you how that works later, so keep reading!

Pitfalls to Avoid

Let's finish this chapter with some pitfalls you want to avoid when lending your hard-earned money.

Don't Invest With Someone Who Lacks Character

In all my years of business, the one that hurts me the most is getting burned by someone who doesn't do what they say they're going to do, especially when they, themselves, are faced with some kind of adversity in their business.

When the going gets tough, the tough work their behinds off to fight through things, but the one who lacks character has already dropped everything and run.

Unfortunately, no matter how much you protect yourself and reduce your risk, someone can always mess it up.

Of course, the challenge is how can you determine if someone lacks character?

This may be a difficult task without knowing someone for 20 years, and there are some tell-tale signs which you should pay attention to.

First, pay attention to how they talk.

- When you ask them questions, are they ambiguous, indirect, or non-specific, or are they confident, strong, and direct?
- Are they avoiding answering your questions, or are they taking the time to explain things thoroughly to you?
- Do they not know the answers to your questions?
- Do you feel like they are only agreeing with everything you say to appease you, or are they answering openly and honestly, regardless of whether it may deter you or not?

Next, pay attention to how they look and act.

- Do they seem antsy, nervous, or defensive, or are they confident and relaxed?
- Do they get upset, rude, or angry when you ask more questions about them or their process, or do they answer patiently and ask for even more questions?
- Do they even have a process, or do they sound like they have no idea what they're doing?
- Are they too arrogant, forceful, or condescending?
- Do you feel like they are trying to manipulate you?

After you talk to them (or even before), Google them.

In today's age of technology, anything and everything is on the internet. Some of it's even true!

Remember, Abraham Lincoln once said, "Don't believe everything you read on the internet."

I saw that one on the internet! Of course, it wasn't even around when Abraham Lincoln was alive. Even so, it made me laugh.

Now, back to Googling.

If something is wrong, it's pretty easy to find out. The person may have a ton of complaints from past customers and clients.

You can search the Better Business Bureau for their company and see if there are any complaints.

I would even connect with them on social networks (or find them on it) and see what kind of posts they share. This is the same thing police authorities do when looking at potential criminals.

If what they post is completely opposite or not in alignment with your beliefs, then maybe you shouldn't be working with them.

If all they share is hate speech, then again, maybe not the best person to work with.

Employers have turned down applicants because they found pictures of them partying all the time, getting drunk, and passing out.

While people make mistakes, repeated action leads to certain behaviors, and those behaviors are the basis of a person's character.

The opposite is also true.

More importantly than their own posts, what do other people post about them? Do people have good things to say to them? Do they interact with others online?

Realize that sometimes, social media is a generational thing. I know many professionals that are of the highest quality and character who don't even touch social media. Yet, you can find a lot of reviews about them or their companies.

And finally, ask for referrals.

Word of caution, referrals are people who the

other person handpicked. So even if they give a glowing review, it may just be a good friend or someone paid to give a good review.

As with anything, you should only base your thoughts upon a combination of factors.

Just because someone has a couple of bad reviews or comments online doesn't mean they are a bad person. Maybe it's just a disgruntled employee who wanted to give the company a bad review or an unreasonable client who was unsatisfied regardless of how good the product or service was. As the saying goes, "haters gonna hate!"

It goes both ways, though. One or two glowing reviews do not mean they are a good person.

The true test of a person's character is what they do when faced with adversity and how they go through it. If you can figure that out, then that's a great indicator of that person.

If you find someone of high quality that you'd like to work with, then avoid this next pitfall of private lending...

Never Send Money Directly To An Individual

If someone asks you to send money directly into their own personal or business checking account for them to buy, fix, and flip real estate – or for some other investment, then that's a red flag!

This tells me that the person either has no idea what they are doing, has no process or system in place to protect their investor, or is planning something nefarious.

Once you send your money to someone directly, there are no guarantees they'll give it back to you.

When you work with me, you will only send money to my attorney's escrow account.

Everything is above board. I can only access your money once the closing is complete and you've been protected with the appropriate paperwork.

This is all part of the step-by-step process I use to protect my private lenders.

I also use this process to ensure I'm doing the right things at the right times.

It's a proven system that works to keep me accountable and to keep my private lender's funds safe and secure.

Speaking of safe and secure, the next pitfall you

have to avoid is not having the right paperwork!

Make Sure You Have The Right Paperwork

I give all my private lenders five things to ensure their funds and investments are safe and secure.

I'll go into detail about each one of these documents and why having them is important to ensure the safety and security of my private lender funds, and here they are:

1. The CMA or BPO
2. The Promissory Note
3. The Deed of Trust (Mortgage)
4. The Insurance Policy
5. The Title Policy

Each one of these documents plays an important role in securing your funds. If an investor doesn't give you all these documents, then they're not doing everything they can to protect you, or they just don't know what they need to do to protect you.

Make sure you, as the private lender, get these documents so that your money is safe and secure.

When it comes to the safety and security of your capital, it boils down to knowing the person you're working with and making sure you have the right documents.

You'll get to know me more and more as you read this book, and for now, you know which documents you need for your protection.

As G.I. Joe says, "And knowing is half the battle!"

And you'll know a lot more after you complete this book, as I'll cover many more questions, concerns, and highlights of private lending throughout it. So, let's keep on going!

"Having money make sense and having sense makes money."

-- Unknown

Why Would You Want To Be A Private Lender?

Great question, right? Really, why on God's green earth would you want to give me hundreds of thousands of dollars, if not more? Well, there's a handful of reasons, so let me tell you why...

The first reason is that you will safely earn a lot more money than you can through any other additional resources or strategies.

You Earn High Rates Of Return

Do you have any idea what kind of interest Certificates of Deposit are getting these days? Go to http://www.BankRate.com and check it out.

Oops... I already spilled the beans earlier, didn't I? At the time of this writing, the average Jumbo CD rate was 1.24%. And that's for a Jumbo CD, which means you have to have a minimum of $100,000 in a CD. If you have less than that, the rate is even less!

Let me clarify in case you don't see that decimal point. That's one-point-two-four-percent (1.24%) or BARELY OVER 1%. It's like a quarter of 1%. Meaning over the course of 1 year, if you have a $100,000 CD, you'll earn a whopping $1024!!!

```
$100,000 .00
x         1.24
----------------------
$    1,240.00
```

These are the kinds of piddly returns most people using conventional means are getting on their money!

By the way, did you know that CDs actually have a negative return when you factor in taxes and inflation?!? The banks are actually charging you to loan them your money! And forget about inflation! The annual inflation rate in December of 2021 is a whopping 7%!! The highest since 1982! And it's only getting higher!!!

For the past ten years, it's been, on average, about 2% - 3% (see the chart below). So, if you only earn 1.24%, you're losing money! In 2022, inflation was 8%! That means you lost 6.76% of every dollar you had!

Year	Jan	Feb	Mar	Apr	May	Jun	Jul	Aug	Sep	Oct	Nov	Dec	Ave
2023	*Avail. Feb. 14*												
2022	7.5	7.9	8.5	8.3	8.6	9.1	8.5	8.3	8.2	7.7	7.1	6.5	8.0
2021	1.4	1.7	2.6	4.2	5.0	5.4	5.4	5.3	5.4	6.2	6.8	7.0	4.7
2020	2.5	2.3	1.5	0.3	0.1	0.6	1.0	1.3	1.4	1.2	1.2	1.4	1.2
2019	1.6	1.5	1.9	2.0	1.8	1.6	1.8	1.7	1.7	1.8	2.1	2.3	1.8
2018	2.1	2.2	2.4	2.5	2.8	2.9	2.9	2.7	2.3	2.5	2.2	1.9	2.4

* https://www.usinflationcalculator.com/inflation/current-inflation-rates

So, what really are most people supposed to do? Unfortunately, they don't know! They aren't taught this stuff in school! Where on earth are they supposed to put their hard-earned money so that they get a great return?

Most people don't have any idea where to turn or what to do ... and that's where I come in. Depending upon the situation, I pay my private lenders anywhere between 5% - 10%. That's **a whole lot more money** than you will get through a Certificate of Deposit.

Let's take a look at that.

If you had $100,000 in a bank or CD earning 1%, that means after one year, you would have earned $1,000!

Nice! That's NOT EVEN a new iPhone.

Now if I paid you 5% interest on that $100,000, then after one year, you would have $5,000! At 10%, that would, of course, be $10,000!

Which would you rather have, $1,000 (or part of an iPhone), or what I would offer you, $5,000, $6,000, $8,000, or $10,000?

I think the answer is pretty obvious.

By the way, why do I offer between 5% - 10% instead of just a flat rate?

Well, we can discuss that in person, and in a nutshell, it all depends upon the amount of money you're lending, the time frame it's available, and the lien position you'll be placed in. Again, when we get together to discuss your specific situation and availability of funds, we'll come to an agreement that works for both of us.

For now, imagine if you stayed as my private lender year after year, deal after deal, for the next five years earning 5% interest.

At the bank, after five years of COMPOUNDED interest, you would have earned a total of $1,256.27

Initial Balance
$ 100,000

Interest Rate
0.25%

	Year End Balance
Year 1	$ 100,250.00
Year 2	$ 100,500.63
Year 3	$ 100,751.88
Year 4	$ 101,003.76
Year 5	$ 101,256.27

Working with me as a private lender, after five years, you would have earned $5,000 a year for five years, or $25,000!!

That's a difference of... well...

A Lot Of Money!!!

That's almost 20 times more than keeping your money in a Jumbo CD. Way more than if it was in a regular 1-year CD or a savings account!

Recently, I had a private lender wire $120,000 to my real estate attorney for a deal - that money was in a checking account. It had been sitting in their bank for 45 days, earning nothing.

Now that they've lent me that money to do a deal, they're going to earn 8% interest on that money - that's an infinite amount of increase over what that money would have done for them!

Many people don't know that an individual can use their IRA, 401(k), or ROTH to lend as private money. I, myself, converted my own IRA into a self-directed one and became a private lender.

In fact, up to half of my private lenders are investing their IRA retirement money with me. Until I told them, not one of them knew that they were able to lend money in this way and double or triple their returns.

It's my obligation to educate the men and women in my warm market - my friends, family, and associates - about the huge blessing they can receive through the magic of becoming a private lender.

Your Investment Is Safe And Secure

The second reason to become a private lender is that it's a Safe and Secure Investment.

The first reason you want to become a private lender is the huge returns you're going to receive on your money but has anyone ever told you that to get huge returns, you have to take huge risks?

Well, don't believe everything you hear!

Let me show you how your investment as a private lender (when working with the right investor) can be safe and secure. First, it is secure because we're not borrowing unsecured money.

What I mean by that is that everybody will get a mortgage or deed of trust, which will back the note. This is the same thing a bank does; it secures real property for your protection.

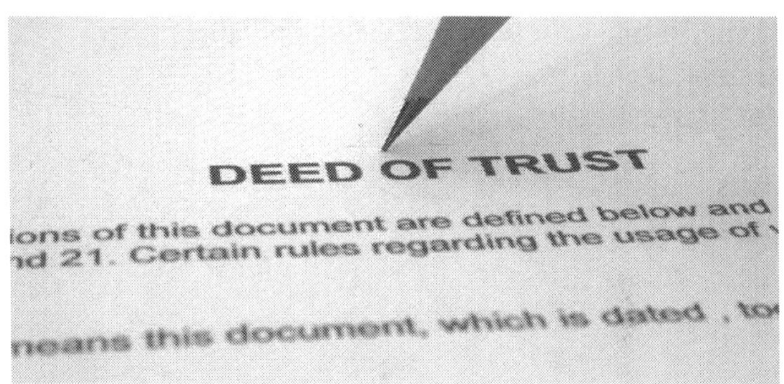

Just to make this brain-dead simple, it means that if something happens to me, you can acquire the property that is used as collateral.

You get the house!

An unsecured loan is like a credit card.

If you spend a lot of money on a credit card and don't pay it back, the credit card company cannot seize your house. They can't take your car, your home, or any of your possessions.

Sure, they can sue you and get a judgment, but then they have to go after you and try to collect what you owe them.

By the way, I don't recommend you spend a lot of money and not pay it back.

Life happens, and due to unforeseen circumstances, sometimes you get behind on payments, and it's always best to stay on top of your bills when possible.

Regardless, since the money I receive from my private lenders is collateralized or secured by real property (a house), then if anything happens, they can acquire that asset (house).

Now, let's be clear, I will always pay them back unless something, God forbid, happens like I get hit by a bus, and I am unable to pay them back.

If something does happen, then they could get the house itself via the foreclosure process. They could then fix it, sell it, and make even more profit themselves!

And the reason they can make a good profit is that I only use a very conservative loan-to-value deal.

Typically, the maximum loan-to-value I borrow is 75% of the after-repaired value. However, I may go up to 85% on rare occasions, and that's only if there's enough equity available to justify that percentage (more on that later in the book).

So, as a result, the private lender has a good equity cushion. In other words, there's enough meat on the bones to keep their investment safe and secure.

To recap, your money is safe and secure because it's collateralized and insured (I'll go into this more in a bit). In addition, I typically only borrow up to 75% of the after-repaired value, leaving meat on the bone in case something ever happens to me.

No Volatility

The third reason you want to become a private lender is that there is no volatility in the value of your investment when you do business with me.

What I'm going to compare this to is the stock market.

When someone invests in the stock market, an individual stock, mutual funds, or whatever, they've already lost money. They've already lost money because they've got to pay commission fees, management fees, account fees, and whatever fees the brokerage account decides it wants to charge you! And that comes off the top!

But let's talk about the market for a little bit. Nasdaq Stock Market was at 5,000 in the year 2000. Fifteen years later, the Nasdaq Stock Market was at less than 5,000. So that means there has been ZERO return over those 15 years.

Think about it.

If a private lender had invested $100,000 back in 2000 in the Nasdaq, that $100,000 would be worth slightly less than $100,000 15 years later.

But that's not all!

The scariest part is that they would have had to watch their $100,000 go down by 70% before it came back.

And if they were like most investors, they would probably have gotten scared and sold everything after they lost a lot of money.

Now let's compare that to investing $100,000 as a private lender at 5%.

That means they would have made $5,000 a

year every single year on top of keeping their $100,000 safe and secure!

If they did NOTHING with that $5,000 a year, they would have earned a total of $5,000 x 15 years = $75,000!

As a side note, that same $100,000 would have only made them a compounded $2,888.22 sitting in a savings account, earning .19% for 15 years.

Now imagine if, instead, they would have lent you that additional $5,000 per year, and you compounded it for them at 5% annually.

WOW! My head hurts!

After 15 years, they would have made a total of $107,892.82 ON TOP of their $100,000 for a total of $207,892.82. More than doubling their money!

Anyway, that's why we use simple interest... to keep everything, well... simple!

And I want you to write this down, the way I do private money, the principal loan amount does not decrease, or rather **the principal loan amount remains the same until cash out.**

What I mean by that is, as the borrower, I am paying or accruing interest-only payments. This means that if I borrow $100,000, I'm making interest-only payments on that $100,000.

I'm not making principal and interest payments.

So, when all is said and done, the payout amount you'll receive is your entire initial investment of $100,000! You get to keep all the interest payments I've made up until that point and get your initial $100,000 back!

Now you see, that's a win for you, the private lender, and a win for me, the borrower.

As the private lender, you'll like and prefer interest-only payments or accruing payments because by making interest-only payments, your entire investment is always earning interest for you!

If I make principal and interest payments, your principal balance will go down with every payment. This means you're not earning as much because not all your money is working for you.

And as the investor using your money, I like interest-only payments or accruals because that helps my cash flow.

For many of my private lenders, this third point is that the private lenders' investment is not volatile, which is extremely important to them.

It's extremely important because many of them may be getting up in years and are elderly.

They need to ensure that they have enough cash on hand for their living expenses in the event that something happens and they need access to their capital.

They don't have time for their funds to take a tumble in the stock market and wait ten years or so for it to recover.

So, they love being a private lender with the knowledge that their principal amount is safe and secure, and they're earning a fixed rate of return without any volatility.

They know that ALL their principal will stay in play, and they'll get everything back when the property sells, along with any unpaid or accrued interest.

It's all predictable income for them.

Why on earth would anyone choose the unpredictability of the stock market over the predictable income of being a private lender?

Most likely because some guy with a logo of a bull on his card or some guy on TV told them that investing in the stock market was safe.

What they didn't tell you was that it's pretty safe for them!

You give them your money, and they make money off of it at no risk, regardless of whether they make you money or lose your money.

They love it!

Unfortunately, they love it at your expense.

Hey, being a private lender is much more simple, more predictable, and safer.

By the way, I hinted at it earlier, and did you catch it?

When you work with me, if you need your investment back EARLIER than the agreed-upon time period due to an emergency, I've got a way to make that happen for you.

I'll go over that in detail when I discuss what a private lending program should contain later on in this book.

For now, let's move on to the next chapter...

"My advice would be to invest in tennis balls... they have a high rate of return."

-- Author Unknown

Why Can I Give A Private Lender Such A High Rate Of Return?

I get it! You're thinking, "Come on, how can you afford to pay your private lenders 5%, 8%, or even up to 10% interest safely and securely?"

Well, I've got 4 big reasons for you.

1. I Buy at 50% of the Value
2. There is No Middle Person
3. I Sell at Full Appraisal Price
4. I Get Properties Occupied Fast

Let's dive into each one in a bit more detail.

I Buy at 50% of the Value

This is a question I get quite a bit from private lenders. How can I pay such high rates of return? If you recall, in the introduction, I mentioned that I'm looking for off-market deals at a huge discount. And I have several ways of finding and working with homeowners to purchase their homes at these huge discounts.

These huge discounts are one of the primary reasons I can pay such high rates of return.

Remember, I'm buying properties at around 50 cents on the dollar. That means that if the house is worth $100,000, I'm typically buying it between $40,000 - $60,000 all in.

Maybe I'm buying it for $40,000 and putting in $20,000 to fix it up. In that case, I'd need to borrow $70,000 (remember Murphy? I always borrow just a little more than necessary in case Murphy visits).

Now, let's say that it takes me a whole year to buy, fix, and sell this property. Of course, sometimes it may take much less, and sometimes it may take a little longer, and for the simplicity of this example, let's just say it takes a full year.

Over the course of an entire year, let's say for various reasons that I'm paying them 8% simple interest.

So, let's do the math...

$70,000 borrowed x 8% interest =
$ 5,600

So, my private lender would make $5,600 on their $70,000 loan to me.

Now, if I sold that house at the after-repaired-value of $100,000, what does that leave me?

$100,000 Sales price
- $40,000 Purchase Price
- $20,000 Repair Costs

$ 40,000 Profit!

Now I have to subtract the fees, right?

$ 40,000 Profit
- $ 5,000 Real Estate Commissions
(if I use an agent to sell)
- $ 2,500 Closing Costs
(I'm being generous here)
(Attny, docs & title fees, etc.)
- $ 5,600 Interest Payments to my Lender

$ 26,900 NET Profit!

In this small example, after all, fees and expenses, I can still make $26,900.

And because I know some of you are thinking, "Wait, didn't you borrow $70,000? When did you pay that back?"

Ha, ha, ha, ha! I know math can be confusing sometimes. And remember, when I sell the property, I actually get a check for $100,000 minus fees.

Taking the example above, the check I would receive from closing is actually as follows:

```
  $100,000 Sales price
- $  5,000 Real Estate Commissions
           (if I use an agent to sell)
- $  2,500 Closing Costs
           (I'm being generous here)
           (Attny, docs & title fees, etc.)
------------------------
  $ 92,500 Check made to me at closing
```

From that $92,500, I pay back my lender their principal and interest:

```
  $92,500 Check
- $40,000 Loan amount used for purchase
- $20,000 Loan amount used for repairs
- $  5,600 Interest Only payment
------------------------
  $26,900 Profit!
```

But wait!!! That means I only paid the private lender back $60,000 in principal and $5,600 in interest.

That's only $65,600!!

Didn't I borrow $70,000?!?!

An extra $10,000 for our friend Murphy?

Am I trying to pull a fast one here?!?

Of course not!

Fortunately, in this example, our friend Murphy did not visit.

So, I never used that extra $10,000!

And because I didn't use it, it's been sitting in my business checking account all this time!

So, in addition to the $65,600 above, I can now return the extra $10,000 sitting in my account back to the private lender for a total of $75,600!

And for all you math people, here's how the private lender funds were used and returned:

$70,000 Borrowed for one year.

Paid back to the private lender:

$40,000 Purchase amount
$20,000 Repair Costs
$10,000 Set aside for Murphy
$ 5,600 Interest Only payment

$75,600 Paid back to the Private Lender

Whew!

For all you non-math people, just know that since I buy properties at around 50 cents on the dollar, there's plenty of spread available for me to pay a high rate of return to my private lenders while enjoying a nice profit for the fruits of my labor.

The homeowner that sold me the property is happy as they were in distress.

I'm happy because I get a great deal and close quickly.

And my private lenders are happy as they earn a high rate of return safely and securely.

It's a beautiful thing, this world of private lending!

There is No Middle Person

Another reason I can offer my private lenders a high rate of return is that they are direct to me.

In other words, there are:

- No Brokers Involved
- No Middle Person
- No Origination Fees
- No Points
- No Documentation Fees
- No Garbage Fees

All these "fees" eat into eventual profits, which are used to pay high rates of return. When working directly with me, there are no fees. Therefore, it allows me to pay out these high returns.

There are closing costs and document fees associated with a closing, and not to worry. I pay all those fees. As the private lender, you don't have to pay any fees whatsoever.

I just tell you when and how much to wire over to my attorney escrow account (remember, you never send money to me directly), and in return, you'll receive a set of documents that will protect your investment.

When all is said and done, I will send you a check with your interest earnings and your full initial principal amount. As my friend's son likes to say, "Easy peasy, lemon squeezy!"

I Sell At Full Appraisal Price

The next reason why I can pay my private lenders high rates of return is that I sell my properties at full appraisal price, and in this hot market right now, sometimes above appraisal price.

Quite frankly, in any market, people are always looking for fully-rehabbed, move-in-ready properties. When a property looks good inside and out, especially in this market (at the time of this writing), it will get multiple offers. And, of course, we're going to sell to the most qualified buyer with the highest offer.

But what happens when the market cools down? How am I going to sell it at full appraisal price?

I'm glad you asked. Well, you didn't really ask, and you might have been thinking about it. So, let me answer that even if you didn't ask yet.

I was taught long ago that you should always have multiple exit strategies for any purchase. And so, one of the methods I use to sell a property is what is called rent-to-own or lease-purchase, or lease-option. You may have heard of one of those terms.

While I won't go into every detail of this strategy, just know that there's always a fairly high percentage of people that cannot go to the local bank and get a mortgage.

Maybe they have bad credit or haven't been in their job for more than two years. Whatever the reason, if they attempt to qualify for a bank loan, the bank will say, "Nope. You're not good enough for us to lend you money."

Well, alright, they might not say that exactly, and sometimes it might feel that way to someone who wants to buy a house and has been to 5 banks who have all said no.

Specifically, NerdWallet says, "The top three reasons for denied applications were:

1. Debt-to-income ratio (cited in 35%);
2. Credit history (22%);
3. And Collateral, or loan-to-value ratio (18%)."

Of course, many of these people still want to own a home, and a rent-to-own type program is just the blessing in disguise that they need.

Some of the people I've worked with in the past are divorcees. Divorce is one of the 5 D's of Tragedy, which I'll cover later on in this book.

Going through a divorce can be a gut-wrenching experience that really messes up your credit and finances. A bank won't touch you for sometimes several years!

And, if they have a good job they've been at for a while, can afford a consideration payment for the option (similar to a down payment when buying a house), and pass a few other checks, I'd gladly accept them into my rent-to-own program.

In addition, as I'm offering these individuals an opportunity to own their own homes, a chance they would not get anywhere else, they're more than willing to pay full appraisal price, and again, sometimes even more... regardless of whether it's in a slow market or not.

Remember the quote by Zig Ziglar? Here it is again, "You will get all you want in life if you help enough other people get what they want."

A lot of times, real estate investors get a bad rap. Some people believe we're just out to take advantage of others, but they don't understand what we do. But I'll tell you this - if a deal isn't a win for the seller, a win for the buyer, a win for the private lender, and a win for me, I'm not doing the deal!

I'm proud to be a real estate investor because I can make a huge difference in the lives of others.

I'm a problem solver - the seller has problems (debt, credit, etc.), the private lender has problems (money sitting around and not earning anything), and the buyer has problems (locating a beautiful, comfortable, yet affordable home).

With one deal, I can solve all those problems. That's why I love what I do and love working with the kind of people who also have a servant's heart. We get to change people's lives for the better. It's a beautiful thing!

I Get Properties Occupied Fast

It's really unfortunate the number of people who want to own homes but cannot qualify for a mortgage, especially in today's economic times. Of course, that's where I come in by offering nice homes on a rent-to-own program.

When I offer a house up for my rent-to-own program, I'm often flooded with people's requests. And when I say flooded, sometimes it's hundreds of people asking for more information about one house. My job is to go through those hundreds of interested people and find the best one for the house.

And if you're currently a real estate investor thinking about becoming a private lender, you can appreciate the next piece I'm going to share. Most investors are taught two things when running a rent-to-own program.

First, they are taught to find the person with the biggest down payment and accept them as the new tenant-buyer or person who will buy your house. This is attractive because, like a bank, the person with the most "skin" in the game is typically the most qualified. I did say typically.

Secondly, they are taught to find someone they think might not complete their rental period. Or they're trained to find someone who won't be able to buy the property after a year or two.

When this happens, the investor can get the house back and find another person with a large down payment. I know. This sounds horrible, right?

From a business point of view, I can understand it. If your goal is to make a lot of money over and over again, this is the way to do it. But, if you're operating with a servant's heart, this is absolutely the WRONG way to do it.

When I'm searching for a qualified tenant-buyer, then yes, I'm not going to deny it; I'm looking for a large down payment. That helps my cash flow and operating income of my business. I want to get out as much money as possible so that I can do more deals. That said, I'm not necessarily just looking for the largest down payment out of all the applicants.

In addition to some kind of down payment, I'm looking for their ability to purchase the house from me eventually.

Understand that if they're giving me $10,000 - $20,000 as a down payment on a $100,000 house, they want to own that house. So, I want to help them own that house.

Instead of just looking for the largest down payment, I'm looking for the most qualified prospect.

One who I can work with on credit repair if they need it. One who I feel can and will eventually buy the house from me because that serves them. One who is willing to be grateful for an opportunity that they wouldn't have had otherwise to become a homeowner.

And often, they won't have the largest down payment... and I'm perfectly fine with that.

I know this book is titled The Magic Of Private Lending, and I genuinely want to convey that it's possible to do that while helping people.

Business can be so much more than just making a lot of money.

And I hope you can feel good knowing that while you're earning a high rate of return as a private lender when you work with me, you're also helping other people.

Now, it might be obvious as to why I want to work with private lenders, and let me do a deeper dive into the many reasons why it makes sense for me to work with private lenders and pay a high rate of return instead of working with banks and other lending professionals.

So, let's move on to the next chapter...

You Can Be The Bank

"Working with others makes us much more than we could ever become alone."

-- John Wooden

Why Do I Want To Work With Private Lenders?

Before I dive into it, I'm going to give you an interesting statistic right now.

Suppose I am focused on just negotiating and talking to motivated sellers who are not in the multiple listing service or MLS. Did you know that after reviewing thousands and thousands of property lead sheets or information from sellers, **only 13% of those for sale by owners will sell to investors like me creatively**?

Now when I say creatively, only 13% of them will sell to us with terms. Terms are fully legal, creative strategies like using a method called subject-to the existing note.

Selling on a lease option, using seller financing, or the seller carries back a note are several more creative "terms" type deals. These are those "No Money Down" deals you might have heard about on some infomercials, and most homeowners will not do them.

The bottom line, my friends, is that the high majority of off-market sellers will require all the money, the entire purchase price, when I close and buy that property.

So that's why private money is so important for real estate investors like me. Being able to pay all cash to help distressed sellers is critical for them and for me!

Let's look at some other reasons I want to work with private lenders.

Flexibility For You And Me

First, when you become my private lender, we get to decide what works best for us in terms of payments.

As an investor, managing my cash flow is critical for my success. Therefore, depending upon my private lenders, sometimes I make monthly payments, occasionally quarterly payments, periodically semi-annual, and often annual. In several instances, I only make a payment when I cash out of a deal.

When I sit down with you to discuss your situation, we can determine when you need your interest payments and how long you want the funds invested with me. This will help me manage my cash flow while fulfilling your needs as my private lender.

Working together, I can be flexible to see what works best for you and me. However, if I work with a bank, I have to do exactly what they say according to whatever program they may or may not have available. There's no flexibility when working with an institution.

As a side note, there are no fees for you as a private lender to pay! I will pay all the fees for you!

This is a HUGE benefit of being one of my private lenders!

Well, o.k., there might be a wiring fee when you send the funds from your bank or Self-Directed IRA to my attorney for closing, and outside of that, there are no other fees for you to pay.

I pay all the closing fees on the purchase and sale of a property. In addition, I pay (if any) all the attorney fees, realtor fees, contractors, inspectors, etc.

You just wire the funds, get your paperwork from my attorney, and wait for the interest to come in! Easy peasy!

Quick Closings For My Sellers

Here's another big benefit why I want you as my private lender. Having private money allows me to close quickly and give cash to my sellers!

As I mentioned before, many of my sellers just want to get out of their house or want to sell it as fast as possible. Sometimes, they will lose their house due to foreclosure within a week or two! Therefore, it gives me a huge competitive advantage if I can offer to **close in 7 days or less**.

And yes, I said that right - seven days or less.

A lot of real estate investors cannot close in less than 30 days, particularly if they are using a mortgage company.

Using private money, I can literally close a deal in 7 days from the time I negotiate a deal and make the offer, and as a result, I'll get many more deals and more offers accepted. And I also said it with confidence! Meaning that I know I can close!

When I have to depend upon "qualifying" for a loan, or I have to find an end buyer to do a "double closing in escrow" (this is where I'm using the end buyer's money to buy the house that I'm selling to them – another no money down, creative financing strategy), I'm already on shaky ground.

If something happens and I don't qualify, or I can't find an end buyer for my deal, guess what I have to do?

That's right. I have to go back to the seller and apologize for not performing. This means I either have to grovel and ask for more time, or I tarnish my reputation by giving back the property after I promised to buy it.

If I do that enough times, no one will want to work with me! Plus, I'll feel like a big pile of doo-doo.

So, using private money, I can make offers with full confidence that I can close and close quickly.

This means I'm going to be able to help more people, get more deals, and help even more private lenders earn money safely and securely!

Credit Isn't A Factor

Here's another big reason why I want to work with private lenders! There's no credit check! That's right!

In the world of mortgage companies, banks, institutions, and hard money lenders, they're all going to pull my credit.

And if they don't like where my credit score is at, then I won't qualify for a loan! That means no money and no deal!

By the way, did you know that just using the credit that you have can lower your credit score? And sometimes getting more credit will prevent you from qualifying for, well, more credit!

Let's say, for example, that you have two credit cards with a $10,000 credit limit on each card for a total of $20,000 of credit. Maybe on one credit card, you just charged a nice family vacation on it, and it costs you (including round trip airfare for 4, hotel, meals, and entertainment) $7,500.

Well, that's not so bad because you used $7,500 out of the $20,000 total available limit that you have.

WRONG! It's bad, according to the credit bureaus.

Did you know that since you put it all on one card, you've now used 75% ($7,500 out of a $10,000 credit limit) of your available credit or what they call a 75% credit utilization on that one card?

It doesn't matter that you still have $10,000 available on another card. Your score is going to go down.

But wait!!! There's more!!

Now let's say your car breaks down, and you need to charge some car repairs on your card. Unfortunately, it will cost you another $2,000 for the repairs.

And guess what?

The card with the vacation expenses on it has a lower interest rate, so you go ahead and charge it on there.

Now you have a 95% utilization rate, and your score will go even lower!

$7,500 Vacation Expenses
$2,000 Car Repairs

$9,500 Total Charges

$9,500 charged out of $10,000 is a 95% Utilization Rate. The Credit Bureaus hate that!

You would think that they want you to use your credit – and they do – they just want you to pay it off right away!

In fact, credit utilization has levels, and at each level, your score gets lower.

The typical levels are 10%, 30%, 50%, and 85% and higher. And if you go over 100% (say you charged $10,000 on your $10,000 card, and the following month they add $500 in interest, you're now over 100% utilization), well, forget about it!

Your score is now dinged as "over the limit," and you get a negative mark, further lowering your score.

You'd be better off if you charged $7,500 on one card and $2,000 on the other.

Of course, if you split your expenses to both cards, you'd be slightly under 50% utilization on each card and be even better off.

This book isn't about credit scores, though. I just wanted to explain how using your credit could actually lower your credit score!

My friends, let's call them Sally and Jordan. Sally and Jordan were going to buy a house. One of the first things they did was work with their bank to get a pre-qualification letter.

This is a letter telling them how much house they could afford, or in other words, how big of a loan they could qualify for.

Once they were pre-qualified, they worked with a real estate agent and made offers on houses they thought would be great! After several weeks of looking and making offers, they finally got one accepted!

They were both so excited!!!

Everything was moving forward, and a closing date was set 60 days out.

During this time, Sally received an offer from her local dealership for a new car with 0% interest for 5 years! Now typically, Sally and Jordan are the kind of people who would just pay cash for a car and not have to deal with payments.

Looking at their finances, they determined that not only did they have enough money for a down payment on the house they were going to purchase, but they also had plenty for a car if they wanted one.

And how could they pass up 0% interest for 5 years? They weren't really planning on getting a new car; however, they thought, "we're getting a fresh start with a new house. Let's get a new car while we're at it!"

In addition, while they could afford to buy a new car outright, with 0% interest for 5 years, why not just finance the vehicle instead?

So, they bought a new car and financed it at 0% for 60 months or 5 years!

Guess what happened next?!?!

That's right!!

The bank found out that they had financed a new car!

And what do you think the bank did?

That's right again!

The bank said, "Sorry. You can't get the loan now!"

It didn't matter that Sally and Jordan had plenty to pay for the car and the down payment. It didn't matter that everything was already in place and a closing date was set. It didn't matter that Sally and Jordan both had excellent credit. None of that mattered.

The bank held all the strings and backed out!

Sally and Jordan were well-qualified borrowers. But, unfortunately, big banks and institutions don't care. They have a set of rules that they follow and forget everything else.

I can't tell you how many times I've heard other investors telling me that they've lost a deal because they can't qualify for a loan!

Everyone around them is doing deals, and they're stuck!

Stuck with no deals!

Stuck with no one accepting their "loan contingent" offers!

Or stuck because they can't even get a loan!

But working with private lenders, my credit has absolutely nothing to do with getting funding for my deals.

It doesn't matter if I have good credit (which I do), bad credit, or no credit! I can still raise private money and do the deals!!

Why?

Because my private lenders are protected by the property and not my credit situation!

Again, it doesn't matter if I have good credit, bad credit, new credit, old credit, or even no credit.

Everything is based upon the property.

As long as I can find a great deal that protects my private investor and gives us both a great return, I can do a deal. That's why I want to work with people like you as my private lender.

As for my friends Sally and Jordan, luckily, they found an experienced mortgage broker who was able to find them a loan from a private institution last minute, and they were able to save their purchase.

If they didn't scramble to find a qualified broker, and he didn't scramble to find a loan for them, they would have lost their deal and had to start all over again with the purchase process... after waiting at least 90 days for that car loan to be "processed" into their credit score!!

All The Money In The World

Another big benefit for me is an unlimited money supply.

I mean, as of right now, there are trillions of dollars in funding available from individuals and private lenders to fund deals.

How many trillions?

Well, it depends upon which statistic you look at. Let's just say that it's way more than enough for me to do what I need to do.

Where did all this money come from?

It came from the Government printing press!

Big government has become bigger and bigger each and every year.

And our politicians have printed money like there's no tomorrow. All that money has flowed into the pockets of individuals, institutions, and other countries as well.

Of course, the United States is one of many governments printing money like there's no tomorrow. Countries around the world are printing cash without any concern at all. All this money flows in and out of countries, companies, and people's pockets.

While there are trillions available here in the United States, there is actually quite a bit more worldwide. McKinsey & Company puts that number at around $1,540 Trillion in 2020 (a lot more has been printed since then due to COVID). And yes, that's Trillion with a capital T!

Now, I don't need a trillion dollars (of course, I'll take it if someone gave it to me 😊), and there's more money available today than there has ever been in history!

The challenge sometimes is getting access to it.

The reason why this section is titled "All The Money In The World" is because when I'm borrowing money from banks and institutions, there is a limit to my line of credit or the number of deals I can do.

Usually, that number is between 5 – 10 deals, depending on my credit and my income! And regardless of my credit, I'm cut off once I've done 5 – 10 deals!

But when I work with private lenders, I can do as many deals as I want, and I can have as many private lenders as I want.

I am only limited by how much time and effort I put into it!

If I want to continue helping people while growing my investing business, I need access to capital.

And one of the best ways is to help more people earn more money.

In other words, it's by working with more private lenders!

I love private lenders because they have funds, and they want to earn more money safely and securely. They just either don't have the time, knowledge, or energy to invest safely and securely in real estate themselves.

Working with me, they can earn higher rates of return safely and securely, and sometimes just as much or more importantly for them, passively!

I do all the work for them!

It's great for everyone involved!

I Get To Keep My First Born Child

If you've ever bought a house and gotten a mortgage with a bank or institution, they have you sign what seems like 1000 documents.

When I was borrowing money from the banks, I had to sign so many papers! It felt like I was promising my firstborn child to them... or an arm and a leg if you don't have any kids!

I was talking to a mortgage broker friend of mine, and he said that every loan has close to 11,000 clauses in it. He told me that his company doesn't hire new mortgage brokers because if they haven't worked in the industry for at least 3 – 5 years, they will have no clue as to all the conditions that a borrower has to agree to, and they will often mess up the loan!!

Working with private lenders, it's a straightforward, safe, and secure transaction without having to promise anyone's firstborn child!

The process I use is easy to understand, quick, and still protects my private lenders' money.

Their money is safe and secured by a property. So, no matter what happens to me, they can get an asset worth more than what they invested!

It's a win-win for both of us!

If These Walls Could Talk

My favorite reason to use private money is that I can get all the cash I need to succeed!

Let me tell you what I mean.

Well, for starters, if I borrow money from a bank, not only do I have to have a down payment, I can only borrow what they allow – which may not be enough for what I need!

Well, let me tell you if only walls could talk when I buy a property! Unfortunately, they cannot, and there's no way I can know what's going on behind a wall if there are no visible signs on the wall itself!

When it comes to home repairs, often, things are happening behind walls that no inspector, no matter how good they are, unless they tear down the wall itself or open it up, can know what's going on.

You could have faulty wiring, leaky faucets, termites, ants, mold, and many other things that you don't know about.

Sometimes you open up a floor to replace it with new flooring, and POW! You get punched in the face with rotten wood that needs to be replaced.

Murphy has come to visit! Or, as many people call it, Murphy's Law!

Now when borrowing from a bank, this sometimes extra $5,000, $10,000, $20,000, or even $30,000 or more is not accounted for. This means cash out of pocket to repair Murphy's visit, or in the worst case, you lose the deal because you're out of money!

On my first fix-and-flip deal, I was quoted $35,000 in repairs and eight weeks until completion. When we opened up the walls, we found a lot of water damage and basically had to gut the entire house down to the studs. Then we decided we needed to do some extra repairs and upgrades to make the house more appealing.

All said and done, that house cost me $100,000 and 12 months to fix up!!! Add on holding costs and utilities; it was quite the Murphy visit! Of course, that was my very first deal. I had no idea what I was doing either, so it's quite an extreme example. I never want to be put in that situation again!

Now, using private money, I always borrow more money than I need when I purchase a property. This gives me excess cash when I purchase, which I set aside for Murphy if he decides to visit!

Let me give you an example:

Let's say you find a property worth $200,000 when it's all fixed up.

I can get the property for $115,000 because it will need $25,000 in repairs, and it's a motivated seller.

So that's:

$200,000 After Repair Value (ARV)
$115,000 Purchase Price
$ 25,000 Repairs

$140,000 TOTAL Needed

When I go to the closing table, I will borrow $150,000 from one or more private lenders.

Well, that's $35,000 more than I need to purchase.

$150,000 Private Money
$115,000 Purchase Price

$ 35,000 Excess Cash

Remember, I need $25,000 for the repair costs leaving me a $10,000 cushion for overages, marketing, carrying costs, etc.

In other words, I will get ALL that money that I need upfront at closing, plus a little bit extra in case Murphy decides to visit!

Now, remember, when it's all fixed up and pretty, I can sell that house for $200,000. At that time, I can pay back my private lender the full $150,000 that they lent me, and they get to keep all the interest they've earned up until then!

So, in our example above:

I sell the property for its ARV of $200,000.

I pay back the private lender $150,000. Let's say I had closing costs, commissions, fees, etc., of $10,000. That leaves me a check for $40,000!!

$200,000 Sales Price
$150,000 Private Lender Payback
$ 10,000 Expenses and Fees

$ 40,000 Profit (Check To me)

Now don't forget, I paid my private lender some interest payments.

For easy math, let's just say it took me 12 months to complete this entire process. And in this deal, I paid my private lender 6%. That means my private lender made $9,000 for lending me that money.

$150,000 Amount Borrowed
x 6% Interest To Private Lender

$ 9,000 Payment(s) To Private Lender

In this example, my total profit would be

$200,000 Sales Price
$150,000 Private Lender Payback
$ 10,000 Expenses and Fees

$ 40,000 Profit (Check To me)
- $ 9,000 Interest To Private Lender

$ 31,000 Total Profit

And don't forget; I had a $10,000 Murphy Visit fee in there. So, if Murphy doesn't visit, that adds to my profit for a total of $31,000 + $10,000 = $41,000.

If Murphy came to visit, that was money well spent, as I'd still make $31,000 on this deal.

If I were using a bank and not a private lender, I would have had to come up with a 20% - 30% down payment on the purchase, all the rehab costs, and possibly a Murphy visit as well.

This would severely limit the number of deals I could do and, depending upon Murphy, could also jeopardize my results.

That's why I love working with Private Lenders!

Not only could I get a great return on a deal, but I could also help motivated sellers, help private lenders, and of course, improve communities by updating houses.

Everyone wins!

No More Banks

So, if you haven't picked up on a theme yet, it's that I don't have to work with banks anymore!!!

For all the reasons above, I don't want to work with banks, and even if I did, there are just some properties that banks won't loan me money on.

Why won't banks loan on certain properties?

Well, it's usually a combination of two things.

First, the condition of the property. If the property is vacant or damaged, the exact kind of properties that I, as an investor, am looking for, then banks won't give me a loan on them.

And yes, a lot of REOs or Real Estate Owned, which are properties the banks themselves own because they got them through a foreclosure, are either vacant or damaged.

The banks want to get rid of these properties quickly, so they usually sell them to a cash buyer. Plus, they want to avoid taking on the liability of a vacant house or one that needs a lot of repairs.

If I find a bank that will lend me money on one of these properties, they're only going to lend me a PERCENTAGE of the Purchase price. So yes, that means I have to come up with a down payment, AND the repair costs myself.

And secondly, and I already wrote about this earlier, regardless of whether they'll loan on these non-owner occupied / vacant and sometimes damaged houses, if I have a lower credit score because maybe I just maxed out my credit cards for materials and equipment, they won't even talk to me.

So, I want Private Money so I can forget about working with banks because of their crazy strict guidelines.

And The Rest

And hey, there are several more reasons why I want to work with private lenders. They're in this book in some form or fashion, so I'm just going to list a few more right here for you.

- I Can Save Money On Fees
    - No Junk Fees Like Documentation Fees
    - No High Origination Costs
    - No Broker Fees
- I Can Get Better Deals (With Cash Offers)
- There Is No Pre-Payment Penalty
- There Are No Points
- I Get Reduced Closing Costs
- I Get All The Cash I Need At Closing
- And More!

Having been through a pandemic, tons of motivated sellers are struggling to make their mortgage payments and are about to lose their homes to foreclosure.

And unfortunately, many people have lost loved ones and are now having to deal with probate, inherited houses, and vacant houses. And they have no idea what to do. Divorces are on the rise. The economy is struggling, and people are struggling.

It's the perfect storm for real estate, and that's where I come in, and potentially, you, as my private lender.

I'm ecstatic that you are reading this book right now because it will not only explain why I do what I do, it will explain how you can earn high rates of return safely and securely while helping people out of their struggles.

So, one question I sometimes ask is, "when would **<u>NOW</u>** be a good time to be a private lender?" Of course, you know the answer, and the answer is **NOW.**

"Yesterday is history. Tomorrow is a mystery. Today is a gift. That's why we call it 'The Present'."

-- Eleanor Roosevelt

The Best Time Is Now!

There's a saying that goes, "The best time to plant a tree was 20 years ago. The second-best time is now."

The same thing goes for buying real estate and being a private lender!
What do you wish you could have started 20 years ago?

There's a real estate strategy out there called the Armchair Millionaire.

This strategy requires you to buy one property every year for 20 years!

After 20 years, you'll have 20 properties, all cash flowing and having accumulated equity!

This is a simple strategy that is great for kids, and hopefully, it's something they can and will implement it in their lifetime. Slow and steady wins the race!

What about private lending?

Imagine if you could invest $100,000 or more safely and securely for the past 20 years and just let it grow.

Instead of imagining "what if's" from 20 years ago, the best time to get started is right now! I firmly believe that "Now is the best time to buy real estate!"

Having just said that 20 years ago was the best time, this statement might sound confusing, so let me explain.

Now is the best time to buy real estate because I am able to find and buy properties for around 50 cents on the dollar!

And regardless of the times, a fully fixed and beautiful looking house, when priced right, will sell quickly within 30 days or less.

Especially right now, at the time of this writing, fully fixed, move-in-ready houses are flying off the market!

There is a huge shortage of inventory, and people are buying houses like hotcakes!

Sellers are getting multiple offers on their houses!

It's crazy!

Supply And Demand

It's basic supply and demand. There are a lot more buyers than there are houses available.

Now I'm sure the market will cool down a bit, and even if it does, since I'm getting properties for such a good price, I'll still make money, and my private lenders will still be protected. Let me go into more detail for you, so you fully understand what's happening.

When most people want to buy a house, the first thing they'll do is talk to a Real Estate Agent. Once they find an agent, they are comfortable with, that agent will start looking for a property using a tool/system called the MLS or Multiple Listing Service.

This is the tool that agents use to buy and sell all their properties. This is also where what we call "Retail" buyers go. These buyers are willing to pay "retail" or what the property is currently worth.

Right now, there's a limited supply of houses and a lot of people wanting to buy. So, a nice house is getting multiple offers when priced right (and the prices keep going higher and higher). There's just a massive shortage of good houses available right now.

One of the reasons for this shortage of properties is a lack of labor and materials. New home builders are building fewer houses because of a shortage of both materials and good workers.

Existing homeowners are selling less too. Part of that is due to an economic and nationwide shutdown due to Covid. Still, people need to move, so there's a huge demand.

This is good for us real estate investors who know how to find good properties. Unfortunately, it's not so good for the retail buyer or the first-time home buyer just looking for a house to move into.

When will this "hot" market slow down? No one knows; regardless, it doesn't matter when you buy right.

How am I able to find properties at such a large discount? Well, I'd like to say that I'm just good that way. I can imagine my wife slapping me on the back of my head if I said that!

And I'll tell you that most real estate investors would say they've discovered this fantastic strategy, method, or technology (software) that lets them find all these great deals.

Possibly...

It's true that real estate investing has changed significantly since I started and continues to change, as with any business.

It's not wrong to say that new technologies and strategies have allowed me to find, connect, and work with motivated homeowners in ways that were not possible before.

Back in the day, I actually looked at the ads listed in the "Homes For Sale" section of the newspaper and personally called each and every ad.

It took up a tremendous amount of time and produced very few results! Today, you'll have difficulty even finding 'Homes For Sale' ads in the newspapers!

If you really want to know the reason why I can find properties at such a great discount, it's because I discovered something that changed everything about the way I do business.

I mentioned it earlier in the Introduction, and I'll say it again here, because it was a literal game changer.

The Game Changer

When I started investing in real estate, it was because I was stuck in a JOB that I did not enjoy. Then I started doing deals and making good money. I enjoyed what I was doing while building a future for myself and my family. And I discovered that I could keep on doing business and making more and more money, and eventually, like a fun ride, it'd probably get boring.

So, what happened?

What changed?

What changed was that I surrounded myself with the right people, and it opened my eyes to the truth behind running a successful, fulfilling business.

And do you want to know what that truth, that game-changer, is? Then keep reading, and I'll tell you later on in this book.

Ha, ha, ha, ha, ha! Just a little author humor. Seriously, you don't have to wait. Here's the game changer. Ready?

Make sure that everything you do is with a servant's heart.

Remember the quote I mentioned earlier from Zig Ziglar? Here it is again, "You will get all you want in life, if you help enough other people get what they want."

Most people get into real estate investing because they want to make a lot of money. Money so they can pay their bills. Money so they can be financially free. Money so they can retire. Money so they can have nice things. When they look for deals, they're looking at how much money they can make, etc.

When I got started 20 years ago, I wanted to quit my job and do something else. I didn't get started in real estate to help others. I started because I thought I could make enough money to leave my job and pursue my passion. It wasn't about others. It was about me.

And hey, I get it. That's how many of the "gurus" out there teach things. That's how they hook us in and get us to spend thousands of dollars on education and courses.

They dangle the carrot of making huge profits on deals in front of people and tell them to get the best deal they can.

It's all about you, the deal, and how much money you can make.

They may mention that you should see what you can do to help the homeowner in their situation, and they tell you to do that so that you can get a better deal, not really out of sympathy for the homeowner.

And I know it sounds like I'm painting a bad picture of a real estate investor, and that's not my purpose.

There are a handful of bad apples that give everyone a bad name, and for the most part, investors play an essential role in an overall real estate economy.

It was the investor that initially started buying houses again after the housing crash in 2008.

Investors were the ones that launched a whole new television industry with Flip That House, Flip Or Flop, fix this, fix that, and all those television shows.

Investors help beautify a community by buying and fixing houses that no one else wants to touch.

And while it's a subtle difference, embracing a servant's heart while growing an investing business is a game changer.

I want to make sure you understand this, because it's part of the reason why my private lending program is designed the way it is.

It's important to understand the logic behind how it operates.

The 4 D's Of Tragedy

So, let me start by saying that instead of focusing on the MLS or Multiple Listing Service like most retail buyers do when they work with a real estate agent, my team and I look for properties that are not on the MLS or what is called "Off-Market" properties.

And instead of working through a real estate agent, we're looking to connect directly with the homeowner.

One of the most critical factors when working directly with a homeowner, who may or may not even know they want to sell their house, is to find out what's going on in their life that's causing problems. In other words, what I'm looking for is the seller's motivation.

Typically, most of these homeowners are experiencing one of the 4 D's of tragedy in their life. So what are the 4 D's? Well, I'm glad you asked!

In a nutshell, the 4 D's are:

1. Death
2. Divorce
3. Disease
4. Disaster

In each and every case, there is a person in need that I can help out of their situation.

In addition, most of these D's cause a 5th D called Debt.

While the 4 D's cause emotional stress, Debt adds to them in the form of debt collectors, legal issues, and other broken relationships.

In the case of a death in the family, if a house is involved, it typically goes into probate and will eventually get inherited by someone. Often, the heirs (the people who will inherit or get the house) do not want the house.

Maybe the house still has debt that needs to be paid, and they cannot afford the additional payments.

Maybe the house is out-of-state, and they cannot take care of it.

More likely than not, the house has many memories that they cannot cope with.

Purchasing the house from them helps alleviate a lot of pain and depression, allowing them to move forward with their lives.

The same situation arises in Divorce and Disease. Going through a Divorce can be tragic in so many ways.

Not only is there the emotional toll, but the division of assets can also be mind-boggling!

Especially when a couple has been together for a decade or more, and almost everything is shared.

Who gets what?

It's even worse when the divorce is unfriendly or due to someone being unfaithful.

Then it can become a sort of revenge (which is never good) and drag out. Usually, the only ones that win are the attorneys involved.

Disease can come out of nowhere and completely take people by surprise. No one plans for cancer, strokes, diabetes, or dementia. Putting an elderly parent or relative into a nursing home can be devastating physically, emotionally, and of course, financially.

Many people in a medical situation find themselves in some kind of debt and struggling to make payments.

Once again, purchasing the house from them allows them to focus on other things in their lives and not worry about making the monthly mortgage of a large property.

In addition, by working with my private lender to pay them all cash, it gives them some funds to start over or pay some medical bills.

Disaster often comes from natural disasters like tornados, hurricanes, and the like. Sometimes it comes from fire or water damage to the property. Usually, it's pretty sudden and unexpected.

This means that the homeowner is unprepared mentally, emotionally, and financially.

If I'm buying a home damaged from a disaster, sure, I'll have to fix it up; and again, I've got the experience, processes, and systems in place to do that.

Most normal homeowners don't even know how to fix a leaky faucet.

By purchasing their house from them, I'm taking a huge burden off of their shoulders and allowing them to focus on finding a new place to live and start over.

And while the 4 D's can result in some kind of debt, there are also many other reasons which lead to debt. For example, it can also come from a job loss.

Hundreds of thousands of people lost their job during the tech crash in the year 2000. Then again, during the housing bubble of 2008. And yet once again, when the economy was shut down during COVID.

Many of these people had a challenging time finding new jobs. In the meantime, their bills never stopped. With bills coming in and no means of income, many homes went into foreclosure.

Once I can identify what's going on in their life, then I can see how I can help them.

In the case of foreclosure, the first thing I ask them is, "Do you want to stay in your house, or do you want to sell it?"

If they answer they want to stay, then I give them a brochure with multiple different options they can pursue to see if they can stay in their house.

Unfortunately, it often boils down to money they don't have.

I do my best to answer any questions they may have and then work with them to come up with a solution. This typically involves buying their house or taking over their mortgage payments.

The Difference

How is this different than other investors? Well, many investors are taught to just send these homeowners a letter that says, "I want to buy your house."

If they get the homeowner to respond, then they basically just offer them a lowball, all-cash offer. This cash offer may or may not even cover what they owe on the property. It has nothing to do with the homeowner or their situation. The investor is just taught to run the numbers and make an offer.

When you're focused on operating with a servant's heart, the focus isn't just making a lowball, all-cash offer so you can make a lot of money.

The focus is asking, "What is this homeowner going through, and can I work with them to come up with a solution that works for everyone."

Sometimes it works out, and sometimes it doesn't. The big difference is that when it does work out, the homeowners in these situations will often thank me for helping them!

Even though they've given me a great deal, they're usually happy with the end result. They don't feel like I took advantage of them, and they're able to move on with their lives.

What's great is that I can work with them to find out what they really need and make sure we address their challenges instead of just giving them some money and brushing them away.

What's great is that I can work with them to find out what they really need and make sure we address their challenges instead of just giving them some money and brushing them away.

Like most investors, I have multiple ways of finding discounted properties and/or motivated sellers. By operating with a servant's heart, it's opened up doors to be able to work with homeowners who are more willing to work with me.

Think about it. If you're behind on your mortgage payments, and you get 20 people contacting you saying, "I want to buy your house." Who are you going to respond to?

Probably none of them.

Now, what if one of them says, "I want to help with what's going on in your life and see if we can come up with a solution to get you out of a bad situation." Are you more likely to respond to that one person versus the other 19 who only want to buy your house? You bet!

That's why operating with a servant's heart, in addition to the newest technologies and strategies, opens doors.

In addition, once I can help someone in their situation, they will tell other people about it.

In other words, good news spreads. People start to talk about how you help people, and you get referrals to deals you never had access to before.

This subtle game-changing mindset has changed the game of real estate investing for the people I work with and me. It's allowed us to find and buy properties close to 50 cents on the dollar.

And when you buy properties at close to 50 cents on the dollar, even if the market crashes, there's room for recovery, and my private lenders and I are still protected.

By the way, after what happened during the housing crisis around 2008, many things like the Dodd-Frank Act were put in place to prevent a crisis like that from occurring again.

So, while real estate markets will go up and down due to supply and demand, I'm rarely going to borrow more than 75% of the after repaired value because I'm buying at such a great price.

You, my private lenders, and I are ensured a safe and secure investment.

Real Life Examples

Let me dive into some examples that can show you what I mean. Even though I've got many examples of houses, I'm just going to show you a few here in this book. Take for example this home on 103 Donna Drive.

The profit on this house was $36,703! Let me show you how it was done.

First, the purchase price of the property was $84,600 and it only needed $4,381 in repairs! The estimated repaired value would be $132,900 all fixed up and pretty.

The borrowed amount was $16,000 in private money (This was borrowed later on in the process to help with cash flow). That's about 75% of the after repaired value.

Once all was said and done, it was sold for $131,900!

So, let's do the math!

Sold:		$131,900
Rents Received:		$ 7,312
Repairs:	-	$ 4,381
Selling Expense:	-	$ 7,656
Holding Costs:	-	$ 5,872
Purchase:	-	$ 84,600

Profit:		$ 36,703

Of course, the private lender was paid back their full $16,000 principal amount, and they kept all the interest paid on it!

And here's what it looked like all fixed up!

Let's take a look at 1811 Barlow Road.

This nice little house had been empty for about 5 years. I negotiated a purchase price of $90,000 with the owner. In addition, he was willing to finance the purchase for me. In other words, because I was using owner financing, I did not have to go to a bank to buy this house.

He accepted a down payment of $1,500 and a monthly payment of $425.00 per month. This was an equity-only payment, so the $425 per month reduced the financed balance by the full $425 each month!

I sold this property for $110,000 using my work-for-equity program receiving a $10,000 down payment and a $1,000.00 per month payment from the buyer.

This property could have sold for more, however, I helped the seller get rid of an empty house he didn't want and a buyer where the bank would not finance to get into a house. This was a win-win-win situation!

Here are the numbers...

Sold:		$110,000
Rent/DPA		$ 8,700
Repairs:	-	$ 500
Sale expense	-	$ 500
Purchase:	-	$ 90,000

Profit:		$ 27,700

Here are some after pictures.

Here's another house at 512 Drexel Road.

This small house was all funded by taking over the owner's debt, and the eventual profit was $24,900. The house can be big or small as long as the numbers make sense.

While I prefer to purchase decent homes in decent areas, I can use this private money strategy to buy a $50,000 house in the country side or a $500,000 in a bubbling metropolitan area and still make it a win-win-win situation for everyone.

Remember, you make money when you buy!

Sold:	$110,000
Rents Received:	$ 3,600
Repairs:	- $ 1,000
Selling Expense:	- $ 1,700
Purchase:	- $ 84,000

Profit:	$ 26,900

And of course, the after pictures....

As I mentioned, you make your money when you buy, and now is the best time ever to buy since so many people are struggling! And for me to buy more, I need more private lenders.

More importantly, running a business with the right intent is a game changer and has opened doors previously unavailable.

When you get to know my team and me, you'll understand exactly what I'm saying and want to be a part of it as well.

Alrighty then!

Let's move on to the next chapter...

You Can Be The Bank

"Having money make sense and having sense makes money."

-- Unknown

Where to Get the Money To Lend For High Rates Of Return?

That literally could be the million-dollar question! And you do not need a million dollars to get started!

How much money do you need to get started?

Well, that depends upon who you're working with.

I'll tell you all about my program later on in this book, and in the past, I've had private lenders starting at $10,000!

Depending on your situation and ability to access liquid funds, you may want to start with a lot more.

Some private lenders start investing with several hundreds of thousands of dollars because they know their money is safe and secure, earning them a high rate of return.

Where do they get it from, and where would you get it from?

You'd be surprised to find that there are so many different sources you could tap into to find money to lend out!

Some sources are relatively well-known, while some might surprise you! To make it easier, I've broken these sources into two categories.

The first category is common sources of funding that pretty much everyone has heard of and knows about.

The second category is, of course, not-so-common sources of funding which many people have heard about but never thought about using!

Let's dive into these two categories and, more importantly, the sources in those categories.

Common Sources Of Funding

Here's a short list that may pop into your head as you think about where to get the money:

- Checking Accounts
- Savings Accounts
- Certificates of Deposit or CDs
- Money Market Accounts
- Investment Capital
- Cash (Under The Mattress Money)

Checking and Savings Accounts

Most people are familiar with those sources listed above especially checking and savings accounts. Unfortunately, this is where most people keep their money.

This is unfortunate because most checking accounts will earn you absolutely nothing. And what's more, many of them have all kinds of fees! You really don't want money in a checking account unless you plan to use it immediately.

Checking accounts go hand-in-hand with savings accounts. Remember how much interest you'll earn in a savings account, though? I told you earlier in this book, and as a reminder, right now, less than a quarter of 1%!

Maybe you could have earned 3%, 4%, or even 5% a few decades ago. Those times have long since passed. Instead of earning a measly

.19%, wouldn't you rather make 35x that at 7% or even more? You can as a private lender!

Certificates of Deposits or CD's

Let's not forget about the Certificate of Deposit or CD. Again, earlier in the book, I mentioned the current national average of around 1% or $1,000 for every $100,000 you invest.

Lots of private investors have CDs that mature, and instead of putting them back into another CD where it's stuck for 1, 5, 10, or 30 years at very low-interest rates, they cash out of those CDs and invest as a private lender for much, much higher returns!

Money Market Accounts

A money market account is almost like a checking and savings account combined.

This means you can spend the money in the account, and it earns a very low-interest rate while it's sitting and waiting to be used.

A prime example of a money market account is putting money in a brokerage account. You use the money in a brokerage account to buy stocks and mutual funds. Then, when you sell a stock or mutual fund, the gains (or losses) go back into your money market account.

While it's sitting there waiting to be deployed, it earns a money market account rate. The interest rate you earn will vary depending on where you have it. Since it's basically like a savings account, you typically make about the same interest. In other words, very little to almost nothing!

Investment Capital

Investment capital is money you use for your investments. Most people use investment capital to buy stocks and mutual funds. If the stock market is doing great, then you do great.

Unfortunately, the stock market goes up and down, and timing is everything. And if you have the wrong timing, it could take you years and years to recover!

Think about this. You have $100,000 in a portfolio of stocks and mutual funds, and the market suddenly decides to sell off for any number of reasons... like, say, a pandemic.

If your $100,000 drops to $70,000, that's a 30% drop. How much do you have to earn to make up that difference?

Well duh. $30,000, of course. But do you know that your $70,000 going up 30% - the exact percentage it dropped - is not enough to make up the difference?

Huh? How does that work?

Well, let's look at this a bit closer. If the market goes up by 30%, then your $70,000 has earned $21,000.

$70,000 x 30% = $21,000

$21,000 you just earned plus the $70,000 that you had is only $91,000.

$70,000 + $21,000 = $91,000

You originally had $100,000.

The market drops 30%, and now you have $70,000.

The market now increases by 30%, and you now have $91,000. However, you're still $9,000 SHORT of what you originally had.

Math is so confusing, isn't it?

In fact, using this confusing math, you'll discover that the market has to go up 42.8% just for you to break even!

But hey, markets don't drop 30% overnight, right?

Well, in case you forgot, here's what happened in March 2020:

- On Monday, March 9, the Dow fell 2,014 points, a 7.79% drop.

- On March 12, 2020, the Dow fell 2,352 points, a 9.99% drop and the sixth-worst percentage drop in history.
- On March 16, the Dow plummeted nearly 3,000 points to close at 20,188, losing 12.9%.

This last drop was so bad that the New York Stock Exchange suspended trading several times.

Let's do even more math. If you had your $100,000 in the Dow, then

- On March 9, after a 7.79% drop, you'd have $92,210.
- On March 12, your now $92,210 would drop another 9.99% and become $82,998.22.
- On March 16, your $82,998.22 would drop another 12.9% and become $72,291.45.

Of course, there were days between those big drops, and what eventually happened was between February 12 and March 23, the Dow lost 37% of its value. So, maybe that's not overnight and that's a pretty big drop in a fairly short amount of time.

And big drops in the stock market don't happen just once in a lifetime. The market has dropped more than 10% in 2022, 2020, 2018, and 2016 – you get the idea! On average, this happens every four years or so; that's horribly often, especially if you like to sleep well at night.

If you cashed out a CD and put $100,000 into the market on January 2, 2020, because, at that time, the market was booming and doing great, within three months, you would have lost almost $40,000.

If you were 25 years old and could ride it out and eventually recover, then that might not be so bad.

And what if you were 60 years old and only had a few years left to make up the difference if you wanted to retire? Maybe investing in a volatile market isn't the best decision.

As a private lender, your money would have been secured by real estate, and your principal amount intact at $100,000 while earning you interest!

But hey, you've got a good financial advisor, right?

They'll make up the difference in no time.

Won't they?

Maybe.

Depends upon the time frame, maybe?!

It's quite funny that several tests have been done with monkeys, darts, and advisors.

The results have varied, with monkeys winning some years and advisors others.

The Oracle of Omaha himself, Warren Buffet, has famously said he would rather give his money to "monkeys throwing darts" to pick stocks and investments than financial advisors.

I'd rather give it to an investor as a private lender where I know my money is safe and secure.

Cold Hard Cash

This leads us to why some people prefer cash to all other things. After all, cash is king!

Most people might think it's silly to keep cash under the mattress, yet some people feel like it gives them a sense of security.

I once met an investor who was looking for a private lender, and he found one just by talking to everyone he met.

Through his conversations, he met a lady who had some money... yep, you guessed it, under her mattress.

By the way, this kind of cash is commonly referred to as "Mattress Money."

And can you guess how much she had under there to give to him? Over $50,000... in cash... under her mattress.

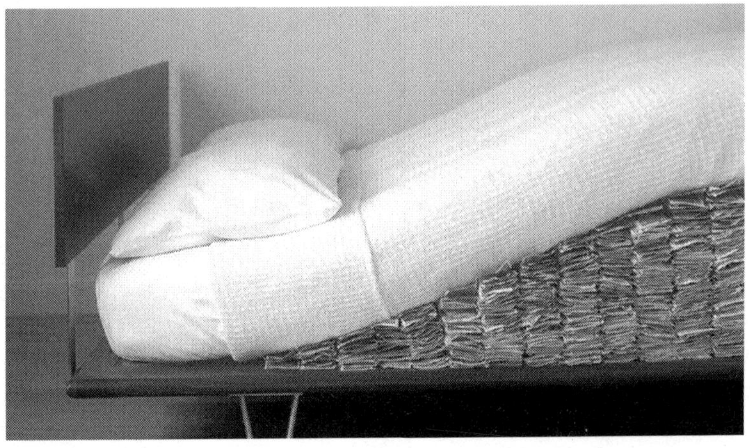

It turns out that she just kept putting money under there and not really paying attention to how much was there. Over the years, it just added up. Good thing for that investor!

The lady just wanted to feel that her money was safe. And while cash under the mattress might make you think that it's safe, it doesn't earn you anything.

Not So Common Sources Of Funding

In this section, I'm going to discuss some maybe not-so-common sources that you may have heard about but didn't know you could access or use to invest with.

Here they are:

- IRA and Retirement Accounts like a 401(k)
- Home Equity Lines
- Portfolio Loans
- Cash Value Insurance Policies
- Credit Cards
- Family and Friends

IRA and Retirement Accounts like a 401(k)

First is what's called IRAs and retirement accounts. Also, let's discuss what is specifically called Self-directed IRAs.

Most people have never heard of truly self-directed IRAs.

Well, what is that?

How do you use the retirement funds that you've already got in order to do business with me on deals?

This is one of the best opportunities I know about out there, and the IRS fully approves it!

In fact, the IRS has approved just a handful of companies across the nation that are called self-directed IRA companies. They are also known as third-party custodians.

These are not brokerage companies that "claim" to be self-directed IRAs. Companies like Fidelity,

Charles Schwab, and Ameritrade all claim to have self-directed IRA accounts that you can use to trade in, and those accounts are not truly self-directed.

You can only buy stocks and mutual funds through them. This way, the broker makes sure to earn a commission from you. In a true, self-directed IRA, you can buy real estate, businesses, precious metals, and more!

The way this works is if you have current retirement funds like a pension plan, a 401(k) from a previous company, an existing 401(k), or any kind of retirement fund, including 403(b) funds, you have the opportunity and option to transfer all or a portion of those retirement funds over to a self-directed IRA company.

Once those funds are moved over, you can direct or invest those funds into any kind of legal investment.

There are no taxes on the funds that you move over, and there are no penalties on moving them over either.

It typically takes 2 - 3 weeks for the move to complete, and then you can truly self-direct those retirement funds as an investment by being a private investor with me and my company.

And here's what's cool. There is no limit to the money or the returns that you can make.

And the money that you can make with your investment with me is at least tax-deferred, if not tax-free (it depends upon the type of retirement fund you've got).

One private lender made $65,000 using his retirement funds in just one year, and it was totally tax-free.

There's no limit to how much you can make tax-free (or tax-deferred).

Here's the bottom line...

If you have retirement funds of any kind, you'll want to have a confidential conversation with me. While I'm not a professional investment advisor, I can answer your questions about this or direct you to the answers to your questions.

In addition, I can introduce you to the representative of the custodian company that I use, and they can also answer your questions.

I've used several companies in the past, and the one I use now is absolutely fantastic! They understand working with real estate investors and private lenders, and their customer service is top-notch! They can even handle talking to your current advisor - sometimes, it's easier to let the professionals handle all the details.

Even though it's your money (and not your advisor's), sometimes your advisor doesn't want to let go of some of it.

O.K. Let's move on to the next strategy to get the money to be a private lender.

Home Equity Lines Of Credit (HELOC)

Another really cool way that you can do business with me, in addition to the other things I talked about, is that you can do this thing called arbitrage, also known as leveraging an asset.

And the way this works is you can use the equity in real estate that you own. It could be in your primary residence, or it could be in other types of real estate. But if you own real estate, you can go to your local bank and get a home equity line of credit or HELOC. And here's what's really cool...

Right now, at the time of this writing, rates are about 5%.

Well, guess what?

You'd get the home equity line of credit and pay the bank only 5%. I would pay you a lot more than that, and you can do what's called "Pocketing the spread."

What's cool about that is this is what is called an infinite rate of return.

You can't even measure the rate of return.

Here's why...

It's not your money that you're loaning out to me!

You're loaning the bank's money out to me by leveraging your real estate asset, and you're pocketing the spread!

How cool is that?

Here's the bottom line for this strategy.

If you have equity in real estate, be sure to talk to me about this opportunity! I'll discuss how you can leverage your asset to make infinite returns safely and securely!

Portfolio Loans

Using portfolio loans is another strategy. This strategy is also a method of arbitrage and infinite returns!

Let's say you own stocks, mutual funds, or both; furthermore, you like your stocks and mutual funds. Since you like them, you don't want to get rid of them yet.

Well, guess what?

You can leverage that asset by getting what's called a portfolio loan account.

Here's how this works...

All you do is contact your stock broker or whoever your representative is where your stocks and mutual funds are located. Once you get a hold of them, tell them you want to open a portfolio loan account.

Now, this is not margin. This is not borrowing on margin. This is opening a portfolio loan account.

And guess what?

You're already approved. There's no credit score involved.

You are approved for a line of credit up to 50% of the current value of your stock or mutual fund portfolio.

It only takes about two weeks or so to get in place.

And once it's done, you'll have a line of credit at your stock brokerage. And the great thing is you still own all your stocks and bonds and continue to get any gains or income from your portfolio.

Interest rates on portfolio loans are about 5% right now. So all you have to do is tell me how much you've got to work with, and I'll go find a deal just as soon as possible.

And then, guess what?

You can pull money from your portfolio loan account and loan it to me on a deal. I'll pay you a much higher rate of return, and you can pocket the spread.

So again, if you like your stocks or mutual funds and don't want to sell them, you can just leverage them and pocket the spread.

Again, an infinite return for you!

Cash Value Insurance Policies

A lot of people don't have any kind of life insurance policy at all, or if they do, they may have some form of insurance through their work. If this is the case, they will most likely have a term life insurance policy.

Since this isn't a book about insurance, let's just say that most life insurance policies are either Term or Whole Life Insurance (or some combination of both).

A Term life insurance policy is just that, a policy that's in place for a limited term or amount of time.

There is no cash value accumulated in a term life insurance policy, and it's typically only used to cover your current debt if something might happen to you.

Let's take a look at an example.

Maybe you own a home worth $200,000 with a $180,000 mortgage on it (in other words, you owe $180,000 to the bank).

You also have a car that you still owe $20,000 on, and you have $25,000 in credit card debt.

In this example, your debt is $180,000 + $20,000 + $25,000, or a total of $225,000.

Assume that your goal is to pay off all your debt within the next 30 years. After 30 years, you won't have any debt. Then it would make sense to get a 30-year term life insurance policy for $250,000.

With this type of policy, if anything should happen to you within the next 30 years, the life insurance policy should pay your spouse, child, or whoever you named as your beneficiary a lump sum amount of $250,000.

This $250,000 is enough to pay off all your debt, and your beneficiary won't be laden with a bunch of loans they cannot pay off.

Your policy will expire worthlessly if you're still alive after 30 years. Congratulations! You're alive! And you just made 30 years of payments and got nothing in return (except, of course, the peace of mind that you're not leaving your family in debt should you die).

This is, of course, what the insurance companies want to happen. They want you to live a long, healthy life if you have this type of policy.
You, too, want the same thing!

This is a "just in case" type of policy and has no relevance to this book! The other type of policy could have plenty of relevance to this book though!

A whole life insurance policy accumulates cash value. In addition, it typically never expires as long as you continue to pay a premium (or monthly fee).

When you pay your monthly fee, part of the fee goes toward insurance, and the other part goes into your cash value in the form of an investment.

Most whole life insurance policies either have a fixed rate of return, typically between 3% - 5% (sometimes more or less depending upon the policy, of course), or they might have a handful of investment options in the form of mutual funds that you can invest in.

The purpose of this type of policy is that after a certain number of years, the policy pays for itself and continues to accumulate even more money all the way until you die.

This is called a "paid-up" life insurance policy.

As it grows and accumulates more cash value, a $250,000 insurance policy may eventually pay your beneficiary several hundred thousand or even over a million more than $250,000 upon your death.

Here's the beautiful thing... you can borrow money from your cash-value insurance policy at a relatively low-interest rate!

But wait!!! There's more!!!

Since this is a loan from your own policy, you don't have to pay any taxes on it. It's a loan. Not a distribution!

And it gets better!

If there's enough cash value in the policy, you'll never have to pay back the loan!

The loan amount gets deducted from the payout amount when you die.

Imagine that!

Getting a tax-free loan that you never have to pay back! What can you do with those funds?

Hmmm.... How about using them for private lending?

So, let's review that again.

You can borrow money from your cash value life insurance policy, never have to pay it back, never have to pay any tax on it, and be able to lend it out to earn a high rate of return.

It's almost like you're creating money out of thin air, and it's all perfectly legal!

In fact, there have been some pretty famous people who have used this strategy to raise money for specific causes.

In 1929, there was a fairly large market crash which then led to the Great Depression.

Many companies went out of business during this period, and many more struggled to survive. One of those companies was called JCPenney.

Like many companies, Mr. Penney had trouble making his payroll and keeping his business going.

His solution?

He borrowed against the cash value of his insurance policy to pay his employees and purchase more inventory.

This allowed him to make it through the Great Depression and continue to grow into a multi-billion-dollar company with over 2000 stores nationwide.

In the 1960s, a fellow by the name of Ray Kroc was busy expanding his budding business called McDonald's.

With cash flow running tight, Ray had to borrow from his cash value insurance policy to pay his employees and fund some marketing campaigns.

Fortunately, this move paid off in droves as today, McDonald's has over $21 billion in revenues with over 37,800 stores worldwide!

And let's not forget about a guy named Walt Disney. Ever heard of him?

In 1928, Walt Disney produced a short film called "Steamboat Willy" starring a character named, "Mickey Mouse." It was a national sensation which then led to several more animated films, including "Snow White and The Seven Dwarfs," "Dumbo," "Pinocchio," "Bambi," and more.

With the success of his films, Walt wanted to create a magical land filled with his characters called "Disneylandia" (later changed to Disneyland). This was going to be an amusement park that was both educational and fun.

With this fantastic idea, Walt took his plan and approached several banks to help fund his dream.

All the banks thought it was a great idea and gave him tons of money to build what would eventually be called Disneyland, right?

Wrong.

Everyone called him crazy and said that his idea would never work.

They said that amusement parks were free to enter, so how could he charge people money to go to his amusement park? No one would show up. They'd all go to the other parks.

Not one to give up, Walt had to find some way to fund his dream. One of those ways was to borrow from his life insurance policy.

Using those funds, he started WED Enterprises (which stood for Walter Elias Disney Enterprises) and launched his dream.

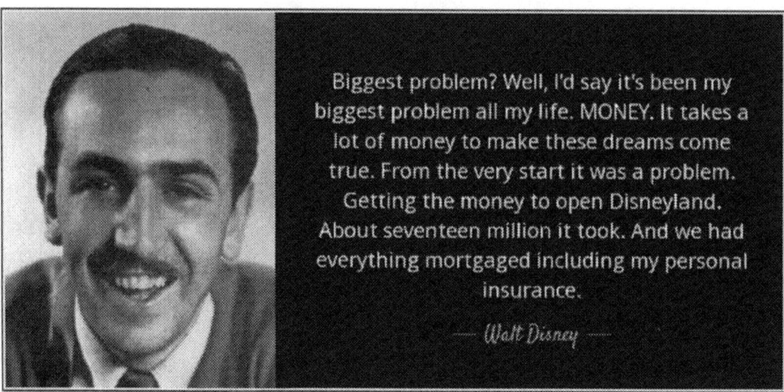

Insurance wasn't Walt's only source of funding.

Another source of funding for him was talking to his friends and family.

They provided him with additional funding as he started the process of building Disneyland.

Wondering if there are any newer examples?

There are!

Doris Christopher started The Pampered Chef with a loan from her life insurance policy. And then Warren Buffet's Berkshire Hathaway paid over $1.5 billion for the company.

Friends and Family

Borrowing money from friends and family can be a touchy subject for some people. It really boils down to two things.

First and foremost, what is your relationship

with your friends and family, and secondly, how much do you believe in what you are presenting?

Many people feel uncomfortable talking to the people whom they think are the closest to them about certain things. It could be due to a variety of reasons.

Ask yourself a question though. "Is what I'm presenting going to hurt or help our friend or family member?"

Then ask yourself, "If I have something that's going to help them and I don't discuss it, am I doing them a service or a disservice?"

Imagine you have a friend you know that maybe has mattress money (you know, that money under the bed earning them absolutely nothing).

You know that they've worked hard and want more in life and just cannot afford it. So, they continue to work hard and put all their extra money under their bed.

What if you can help them earn 3%, 4%, 5%, or more on their money, and they don't have to do anything extra at all?

And what if by helping them, you too could earn 1%, 2%, or 3% or more?

How can you do this?

You can do this by simply borrowing money from them and paying them, let's just say, 5% interest, and then lending it out as a private lender and earning 6% interest.

What happens to that 1% "spread"?

Of course, you get to keep that.

It's a win-win-win situation.

Your friend wins and earns 5% on their mattress money.

You earn 1% (an infinite amount of return for you since it's not your money!) on the spread.

And the investor gets to work on a house that could potentially produce even more wins by helping a struggling homeowner sell their house, improve the community by fixing up and prettying older homes, and help someone buy a home they couldn't qualify for through a bank.

Once again, remember the quote, "You will get all you want in life if you help enough other people get what they want."

It's just so true!

There is a caveat to this strategy. You should only do this with people you already know or have known for some time.

If you go out and start talking to people you

don't know about whether they have money you can borrow and then lend out, you could be considered a "professional" broker.

Professional brokers have different rules and regulations, so keep it safe by only using this strategy with friends and family.

If you do, it will help them (and you), and you'll avoid any kind of regulations about being a professional broker.

So, who do you know that you can help get a higher return on their money?

Credit Cards

Let's move on to the last uncommon source of getting money for private lending that I'll discuss in this book, and that's credit cards!

When most people think about credit cards, they think about buying things. They think about the debt that they have to pay off. They think about... ugh... bills!

When you really look at it though, what are credit cards except another tool to be used for your benefit? Credit cards are just another source of funding for you if you have a good credit score.

Provided you have a good credit score, it's amazing the amount of credit you can qualify for!

Credit card companies will fall over backward to give you their cards. In addition, many of them offer rewards and even cash back!

And the best part, most of them have a low to no interest rate introductory offer. This means you can get 1, 2, 3, 4, or more credit cards with a 0% interest rate for 12 – 18 months!

Imagine getting four different cards, each with a credit limit of $10,000 - $20,000 at 0% interest for 12 – 18 months. Let's say the total comes out to $50,000 in credit.

If you made a cash advance, pulled out all $50,000, and then lent it out as a private lender earning 5% interest, how much would you make after a year?

$50,000 x 7% = $3,500.

Sure, it may cost you a little for the cash advances, and you can still make a couple of thousand dollars with this strategy.

And once again, since it's not your money, it's an infinite return! Who doesn't want infinite returns?

So, there you have it!

Multiple different sources of funding for you to become a private lender.

The key point of all this is to let your money (or someone else's money) work for you!

Think of each dollar you have as an employee.

You can let that employee sit around and do nothing (which is not the best business plan), or you can put them to work.

The more employees you have working for you, the more money you can make – of course, with very low risk.

"Great things are done by a series of small things brought together."

-- Van Gogh

Let's Discuss My Private Lending Program

Are you ready to get down to the details? In this chapter, I will go through my private lending program in 6 easy points.

Before I do that, just a quick disclaimer reminder that this book and the information in this book are not solicitations for a security, fund, or investment. This chapter is simply what I've paid my current and past private lenders and how I work with them.

If you decide you want to work with me, we will sit down and discuss your particular situation.

We would then determine what makes sense for you and me and take the necessary steps to proceed from there.

So, with that said, back to my six points.

I'm super proud of these six points as I believe that they, along with the documentation you'll receive, really make my private lending program stand out among all the other private lending programs.

In essence, being a private lender simply means that you are lending someone your hard-earned cash with the promise of a rate of return.

Not all private lending programs are equal. Many programs are unsecured, and your only security is the hope that whoever you lent the money to doesn't run away with it or make a few mistakes and lose it all.

With these six points, you can go along your day knowing that your funds are working for you every day safely and securely.

So, if you haven't been taking any notes, now would be a great time to start!

Here are the six points I'll be discussing in this chapter:

1. Interest Rate
2. Loan-to-Value
3. Term
4. Payments
5. Early Withdrawals
6. Your Minimum Return

Interest Rate

For all my private lenders, I pay 8% - 10% simple interest, annual rate of return depending upon the deal. This is based upon whether you're in first or second position.

Simply put, I pay 8% simple interest when I use funds to buy a house. In other words, I would need a larger amount of funds to do this. In return, you, as the private lender, would receive a first lien position.

A first lien position means you have the property's greatest protection.

This is typically the position that a bank holds when you buy a house with a traditional mortgage. Remember, a bank is like a private lender, except they are a business and not an individual like you.

The process we follow is exactly the same as what a bank would do.

For smaller amounts of funds, I would typically use it to fix up a property or take over a property using a creative financing strategy.

In this instance, an investor would receive a 10% annual rate of return because they would get a second or third lien position.

Again, similar to a bank, this would be as if you got a second mortgage or a home equity line of credit (otherwise known as a HELOC).

The second mortgage or HELOC would get a second lien position since the first mortgage is typically a first lien position.

So, to review, for larger amounts, if you were my private lender, you'll typically receive a first lien position and an 8% return. For smaller amounts, you'll receive a 10% return and a junior (second or third) lien position.

And because you might be asking, let me just answer it ahead of time, "How many lien positions are there?"

The answer is as many as needed until I reach my maximum LTV to ensure that EVERYONE's money is protected.

This is a great segue into point number 2, the Loan-To-Value or LTV.

Loan-To Value

I structure my deals with protecting my private lenders' funds as my top priority. Here's a simple breakdown of the LTV.

- For deals with an after-repaired value or ARV of $150k or less, I keep the LTV amount to 70% or less of the ARV.
- For deals with an after-repaired value or ARV of $150k to $350k, I keep the LTV amount to 75% or less of the ARV.
- For deals with an after-repaired value or ARV of $350k or more, I keep the LTV amount to 85% or less of the ARV.

Let's take a look at a quick example.

Let's say I find a house at 777 Lucky Street. I work with the homeowner, and the purchase price is going to be $75,000.

After working with my general contractor, we determined that the rehab or fix-up cost would be $45,000.

This means that the total funds needed for this property will be $120,000.

$ 75,000	Purchase Price
+ $ 45,000	Rehab Cost
$120,000	Total Funds Needed

In addition, my real estate agent ran some comparables and determined that once the property is all fixed up and pretty, they could list it on the market and sell it for an After Repaired Value or ARV of $200,000.

$120,000 / $200,000 = 60%

So, the maximum amount of money I would need to buy and fix this property is $120,000, which is only 60% of $200,000.

The LTV for this deal is, therefore, 60%.

The MAXIMUM amount I WOULD borrow is up to 75% of the ARV. Since the ARV is $200,000, 75% of that is $150,000.

$200,000 (ARV) x 75% = $150,000

So, in this example, let's say I find a private lender who lends me $100,000. This is enough for me to buy the property and give them a first lien position.

Since the total amount I need is $120,000, I can work with my friend Alex for the remaining

$20,000.

Alex, by the way, is just another private lender I met through various means. Regardless, he lends me $20,000, and in return, he receives a second lien position.

With his $20,000 and the $100,000 from the first private lender, I have the total amount I need for this property.

But wait! There's more!

Let's say I purchase this property, and when my contractor gets in, he finds out that there is some damage behind a wall that no one could have seen or known about.

So, he needs an additional $10,000 to tear down and replace the entire wall.

Remember our friend Murphy? Seems like he paid a visit.

Of course, as part of my rehab planning, I would have already accounted for Murphy, and this $10,000 should have been already allocated in the budget, and for the sake of this example, let's just say it wasn't.

Fortunately, in this example, I only borrowed 60% LTV. With my program, I can borrow up to 75% for a property of this size.

75% of $200,000 = $150,000.

Since I only borrowed $120,000 in this example, I can borrow an additional $30,000 from another private lender. If I did so, that private lender would then receive a third lien position and get paid a 10% annual return.

To recap:

$ 75,000	Purchase Price
$ 45,000	Rehab Cost
$ 10,000	Murphy's Visit
$130,000	Total Funds Needed

$100,000	From Private Lender 1 (1st Lien Position)
$ 20,000	From Private Lender 2 (2nd Lien Position)
$ 30,000	From Private Lender 3 (3rd Lien Position)
$150,000	Total Borrowed

Again, why would I borrow $150,000 when I only needed the $130,000 in this example?

Because if Murphy decides to visit again, I'll be prepared and won't have to find a fourth private lender to make this deal work.

And once the project is finished, everyone wins!

Terms

My minimum term of borrowing funds is typically 12 months.

For private lenders who use retirement funds, I'll typically borrow the funds for 2 - 5 years, as they usually don't want to touch these funds until they have to for retirement, and 1 - 2 years for private lenders who use funds other than retirement funds. Terms are always negotiable.

Depending upon the private lender and the project I may need funding for, we may agree to have a longer loan period of seven or even ten years. Again, this is ideal for those individuals who have funds that they just don't want to touch for an extended period of time.

A great example of this is Charlotte.

Charlotte is Charlie's mom, and she started a college fund for Charlie when he was born.

Charlotte puts $10,000 each year into Charlie's college fund, so at age 5, Charlie already has $50,000 in his college fund.

As a side note, at today's rates, that's only enough for one year of college. Crazy!

Charlotte wants to ensure Charlie's money is safe and secure, as he'll use it when he gets older.

Since Charlie has over 13 years before he even decides on where to go to college, he's a perfect candidate to be a long-term private lender.

In addition, each year, Charlie will have additional funds that can be put to good use! Then, when it's time for him to go to college, he won't have any issues paying for the tuition!

And, of course, depending upon the private lender, once our agreed-upon term is completed, as long as they are happy with the returns, as most of my private lenders are, and they want to continue, we can always renew for an additional period of time.

Remember, the amount of the principal never changes.

The private lender will just keep getting paid an annual rate of return, typically 8% - 10%, for as long as I'm using their funds.

My private lenders love this because where else are they going to earn a high rate of return safely and securely?

Payments

As far as when I make interest payments, in my program, I offer 4 payment options:

1. Monthly payments (every month)
2. Quarterly Payments (every 3 months)
3. Semi-annual payments (every 6 months)
4. Annual payments (every 12 months)

I discuss this with each and every private lender. My preference is to have annual payments if I'm going to buy a house with private money. This lets me focus on the deal and control my cash flow better.

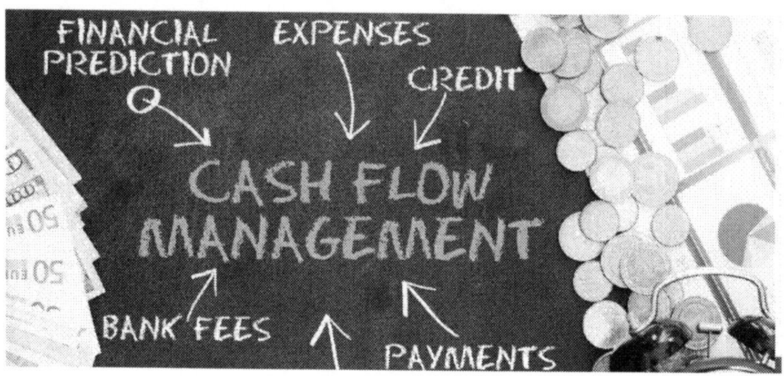

Managing cash flow is critical to the success of every project and my business overall. So, if I can let the interest accrue and pay my private lender out annually, that helps me manage that cash flow.

While that's my preference, I will also work with the individual private lender to meet their needs as much as possible.

In addition, I do not want to accrue more than 12 months or 1 years' worth of interest simply because I just don't want that debt hanging out there for too long.

While managing cash flow is important, managing debt is equally important.

The bottom line is that I will work with the private lender to determine what works for them, and once we agree upon a timeframe, I will schedule payments to go out automatically at the agreed-upon time.

Early Withdrawals

Very few, if any, private lenders I know offer this next point which is an early withdrawal option. While we agree upon a predetermined loan period, I offer a 90-day call-back option for all my private lenders except for lenders using retirement funds.

The 90-day call-back option ensures you will have your funds returned to you within 90 days of your written request, along with any payments owed. The 90 days also allow me to find another private lender to replace the funds you call back.

Hey, I get it.

Life happens.

Sometimes something comes up, and you need

your money back sooner than the agreed-upon term.

My goal is always to lead with a servant's heart and do what's right. This includes getting your principal amount back within 90 days of your request and hopefully sooner.

Unlike a bank CD or 30-year bond, you are not locked into your term if you really need your funds.

Of course, it goes without saying that please don't ask for your funds before the term period is over unless you really need them for something.

This will interrupt the project we're working on together, as I will have to find another private lender to replace your funds and finish the project.

And the fewer the interruptions, the faster a project can be completed so that everyone wins.

Your Minimum Return

Speaking of faster project completion, you're really going to like this next point.

All my private lenders will get a minimum of 6 months of payments no matter how soon I finish the deal, as long as I don't have anywhere else to put the funds!

Let's say we have a note that is set up for three years. So, the term is for three years. And just like when you get a mortgage from a bank, there's typically no pre-payment penalty.

This means that if the loan is paid off early, there's no penalty or fee.

Some banks don't like this because they make money when lending money, and when you pay it off early, they don't make any more money.

Unlike the banks, we promise to pay our private lenders a minimum amount regardless of how soon we pay off the loan, even if it's after 30 days.

Let's take a look at an example...

Let's say you lend me $100,000 at 12% for 2 years to buy, fix, and flip a house. Remember, I typically pay 8% - 10%, and 12% is easier for this example.

Things are rocking and rolling. I finish the deal in 4 months. I borrowed your money for 2 years though. What happens next?

Typically, I would do a substitution of collateral (which I'll talk about in a bit) and put your funds to work on a different property. This would continue to collateralize and protect your funds.

Let's say, for some reason, right now, I don't have any properties available to substitute and collateralize your funds. Maybe I'm already working on three other projects and do not need your funds yet. Or I'm on vacation for a month, and I'm not working on any new projects at the moment.

Regardless, once the property is sold, your lien position will end. This means that if I kept your funds, they would be unsecured, and that's not my program.

I want your funds to be safe AND secure.

In this case, I would have to pay you back your principal and any accrued interest.

Since it only took 4 months, your interest payments should total $4,000 (12% annual interest on $100,000 is $1,000 per month or a total of $4,000 for 4 months).

However, since I promise to pay you at least 6 months of interest, you'll receive $6,000 in interest instead of $4,000!

That's an additional $2,000 in your pocket for doing absolutely nothing!

In addition, you'll have all your funds available when I find that next project to work on. Of course, my goal is to keep your funds working for you as long as possible.

Listen, I know you have a choice of where to invest your money, even if it's a whopping 1%

or less at a bank!

When you decide to work with me, I want to reward you for your decision by making sure you're paid with at least 6 months' worth of interest.

See, I told you that you'd like this point!

All that being said, as I mentioned earlier in the promissory note, I do have the right to substitute the collateral and continue using your funds if I end up selling a property early.

Additional Bits and Pieces

Those six items covered previously make up the bulk of my program. Let's dive a little deeper and answer some additional questions about it. First, let's make sure that you understand what substitution of collateral means.

What Does Substitution Of Collateral Mean?

Good question. Substitution of collateral simply means that if I complete and sell a property 7 months into our 3-year term, then the current lien you have is paid off at the sale of the property. Usually, I would pay you the interest earned for 7 months and be done.

With a substitution of collateral, instead of paying you back your funds right away, I would just give you a new lien on a new property, and your money would continue to accrue interest for as long as I use it.

This is a win for me as I can continue to do more deals, and it's a win for you as your money will continue to work for you without interruption.

In addition, you'll continue to earn a high rate of return on it for the duration of our agreed-upon term of at least 3 years or more instead of just going back into a savings account, earning you 1% or less!

How cool is that?

Am I Concerned About Market Conditions...

... and being stuck with a house and unable to sell it?

And the answer is "No" for a number of reasons.

First of all, we're in a very hot seller's market at

the time of this writing! Anything that's put in the Multiple Listing Service at a fair market price is getting snapped up and usually will receive multiple offers within the first 24 – 48 hours!

Right now, it's a hot market, so I'm definitely not concerned.

But wait! What if it's not a hot market?

What if it's a buyer's market, where there's plenty of inventory, and houses are just sitting there waiting for someone to buy them?

We've had several of these "slow" markets throughout the years. In the '70s, '80s, '90s, and in the early 2000s, we had the big housing bubble.

Well, guess what?

People still needed to move and buy houses.

Kids grew up and moved out and needed places to stay.

First-time home buyers are always going to be around.

Military personnel are constantly moving around every few years.

People entering the job market, switching jobs, or finding new jobs are always moving.

So, there will always be buyers and, of course, sellers.

The key is that I buy properties at a deep discount. In other words, you make money when you buy a house the right way!

After I fix them up and make them look pretty, they are worth a whole lot more, and people love "move-in-ready," fully rehabbed homes! Priced right, even in a slow market, I sell my houses fast.

Now, let's say it's a slow market, and there are more renters than buyers. Well, that's fine too.

I can sell my houses on what I call a rent-to-own or lease-option program.

Even in a slow market, there is always a large number of people or potential buyers who want to own their own homes.

And unfortunately for them, most of them cannot qualify for a loan from a bank to buy a house. Statistically speaking, over 80% of the population cannot afford a home and/or qualify for a loan to buy that home in the United States.

The reasons are numerous and include not having enough money for a down payment or not having good enough credit!

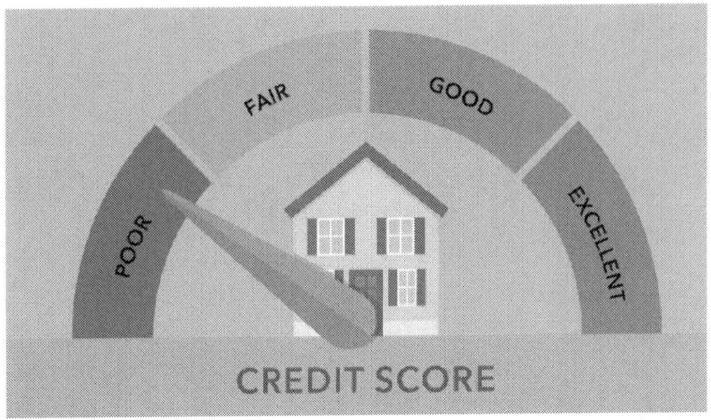

With my rent-to-own program, if someone has bad credit or not enough cash for a down payment, I might be able to work with them if they have a good-paying job and are willing to work on credit repair.

This program allows someone to rent from me for a year or two and then buy that rental property from me at the end of their lease or even before.

And the best part is that I can oftentimes get above market rents which ensures that I can pay the interest that I'm paying my private lenders, as well as any and all expenses related to that house.

In addition, these buyers are not shopping price.

They are looking for an opportunity... one which I can provide them with my programs.

The bottom line is that you are Well-Secured by

a Low Loan-to-Value Ratio, making sure that your investment is safe and secure.

If necessary, when I sell, I could even drop the price of the house significantly, and you would still get all your money back!

Where Does the Private Lender Send Funds?

You wire it directly to the Real Estate Attorney's Trust Account. I always use a real estate attorney for my closings, and they prepare the documentation.

The private lender does not give funds directly to me, the real estate investor. You always send it directly to my real estate attorney's trust account, and no funds are disbursed until everyone is protected and the mortgage or deed of trust is recorded.

Now I do this for several reasons.
First and foremost, I don't want to touch any of your funds!

This is a professional business, and I want the right professional to take care of the right things!

I've met some investors who say to their private lenders, "Sure, send me a check for $100,000. Make it out to 'John Doe'."

You might as well send a check to his Nigerian uncle while you're at it!

Hey, I'm not saying this to knock down other investors.

In reality, many investors do not have a private lending program and have no idea how to protect their private lender's money.

They're so focused on keeping their head above water and just doing deals that they haven't considered all the ins and outs of private lending.

Again, I want a professional to handle your hard-earned cash, which leads me to the second reason why I have you send your funds to my attorney's trust account and not me directly.

You should feel comfortable knowing that your money is safe and secure with a licensed and certified professional handling your funds.

Remember, this entire book is about how you can earn high rates of return SAFELY and SECURELY.

Sending money to an attorney's trust account and not to me, the investor directly, is just another layer of protection for you.

Does The Private Lender Pay Any Costs Associated With Lending Money To Me?

Well, doesn't working with an attorney cost money? Do you have to pay anything to the attorney or anything during the closing?

No! As part of my private lending program, I pay all closing costs to the attorney, and you never incur any costs associated with loaning me money.

You read that right. I pay all closing costs. You pay no costs associated with loaning me money. In addition, nothing comes out of your principal loan amount!

So, when I finish a deal, I will pay back all your principal loan amount (unless I'm substituting the collateral). In addition, I'll pay you any unpaid accrued interest on that deal.

Your principal loan amount invested with me is safe and secure and will never decrease. You'll also know the exact amount and rate of return you'll receive for lending me that money.

Are you ready to become one of my private lenders yet?

What is Your Range of Investment?

Hey, the sky's the limit!!!

I'm always looking for GREAT deals where I can help out a homeowner looking to sell, help potential home buyers find a beautiful home, and be able to employ a bunch of people, including real estate agents, attorneys, general contractors, and their crews. And, of course, help my private lenders earn high rates of return

safely and securely! When I do find a great deal, everybody, and I do mean everybody, wins!

And usually, one of the biggest bottlenecks is having enough private money to do more deals!

So, the sky's the limit to the amount you can lend on the upside.

On the lower end, I use smaller amounts for rehabbing properties.

A typical rehab project can run between $25,000 - $50,000 or more. Usually, I'll need at least something in that range to start working with you.

Usually, I said. The most important thing is that you're interested in working with me.

Some projects may only require a smaller amount as well.

When we sit down and have a conversation, just let me know what you have to work with. We'll see if we can come to an agreement based on what I have available in my pipeline and when you're ready to invest.

If anything, we can sit down and devise a plan

for how we can work together in the future.

And remember, there's an entire chapter devoted to helping you find funds to become a private lender. It might be possible to combine several of those strategies to come up with an amount of funds that works for both of us.

Phillip C. McGraw once said, "Life's a marathon, not a sprint." The same is true about this business.

I would love to build a long-term relationship with all my private lenders, where we all benefit.

So again, if you're interested in becoming a private lender, reach out to me, and let's have a conversation and see where it goes!

You Can Be The Bank

"Yesterday is history. Tomorrow is a mystery. Today is a gift. That's why we call it 'The Present'."

-- Eleanor Roosevelt

How Are You Protected?

This is the super important question that I've touched upon throughout the entire book so far. When I borrow money, my number one concern is to ensure that the borrowed money is protected.

I know not all investors feel this way. Some investors just want to use other people's money and hope everything goes right. That's not enough for me though.

For me, borrowing someone else's money is a responsibility I take seriously. The thought of losing someone else's money hurts me more than losing my own money.

You heard that right. Why is it so important to me?

It's important because you've put your trust in me, and in doing so, I've taken on a responsibility to ensure that trust is well placed. My integrity is on the line. My honor is on the line. And I have to do everything I can to fulfill my obligations to ensure that you can sleep well at night knowing that your money is safe and secure.

Of course, actions speak louder than words, so through my private lending program, I've taken the measures to ensure the safety of your funds.

I'll go into further detail on how all this is accomplished in this chapter, so for now, just know that I don't borrow any unsecured funds. I COULD do so both legally and ethically. With a Self-Directed IRA, you could lend your money out unsecured to almost anyone. Borrowing unsecured funds is not something I do.

Regardless of how much you know and trust me, I want to make sure that all of my paperwork is done correctly. That way, everyone is mentally, emotionally, and legally protected. Earlier in this book, I mentioned that I provide my private lenders with 5 documents to ensure their funds are safe and secure.

Do you remember what those 5 documents are? It was quite a while ago, so here are those 5 documents again:

1. The CMA or BPO
2. The Promissory Note
3. The Deed of Trust (Mortgage)
4. The Insurance (Hazard) Policy
5. The Title Policy

Remember, my real estate attorney prepares all paperwork!

Let's go through them one by one to make sure you understand each document and why, when you work with an investor (whether it's me or someone else), you should verify that you receive these documents.

The CMA Or BPO

Before I dive into this section, let me just say that I've worked with many, many real estate agents, lending companies, and licensed appraisers.

What I can tell you is that it's all subjective!

The real estate agent might think a property is worth $100,000. The appraiser might come out and say, "it's only worth $90,000". And then, the lender will send out their own appraiser and come back with a valuation of $75,000. Talk to another appraiser, and they'll think it's worth $125,000.

What's the difference?

Having been in this business for a while, I've worked with real estate agents and appraisers and even gone through some appraisal training myself. I can tell you that the difference really lies in what they are using to calculate the value if they are considering market conditions, how experienced they are in the industry, and this last one, which is probably one of the biggest reasons why there is a discrepancy between two people – how lazy they are.

I know that sounds funny when talking about licensed professionals, and trust me; some professionals are lazier than others. Because of this, they may not do all the research they need to in order to come up with an accurate value of a property.

With all my properties, I work with an experienced, investor-friendly, professionally licensed real estate agent who is a go-getter to pull together a CMA or Comparable Market Analysis or a BPO or Brokers Price Opinion.

I mentioned a few keywords in there, if you noticed. First and foremost is experienced. I'm always looking for professionals at any level. They just make doing business (and my life) easier. They understand what it takes to get things done and are not afraid to do what it takes.

The go-getter part comes into play here as well.

Have you ever heard of the saying, "the harder I work, the luckier I get?" I find that statement to be profoundly true.

I love working with hard-working professionals who are not afraid to put in the work to get things done right.

I also mentioned investor-friendly.

Yes, I am an investor.

And no, not all real estate agents like working with investors.

And unfortunately, I don't blame them.

I say, unfortunately, because I know there are many investors out there who are only looking to make a quick buck.

As with every industry, it only takes a few rotten apples to spoil the entire barrel.

Investing is a business. And if you want to succeed in any business, you must put in the time, effort, and energy to succeed.

In addition, you must get the proper training and education to succeed.

Those who don't get enough training sometimes make life difficult for themselves as well as the people they work with, i.e., real estate agents.

Therefore, when an investor like me finds a qualified, investor-friendly real estate agent, we tend to stick together, grow together, and profit together.

This leads me back to this section's main point: working with the right people to find the most accurate CMA or BPO possible.

I want to know that I am not overpaying or overestimating property values.

This is critical for several reasons, including the safety and security of my private lender's funds.

So, again, I only work with the highest quality agents to determine property values regardless of what it says a property is worth online at Zillow.com or some other website.

This also adds to the comfort of my private lenders, knowing that their funds are safe and secure with plenty of equity for their protection.

The Promissory Note

Next is the promissory note. The promissory note simply lays out the terms of the note.

This identifies who's the borrower, who's the lender, what's the interest rate, what's the principal loan amount, are there payments, how often the payments are, the length of a note, etc.

It's kind of like your "contract."

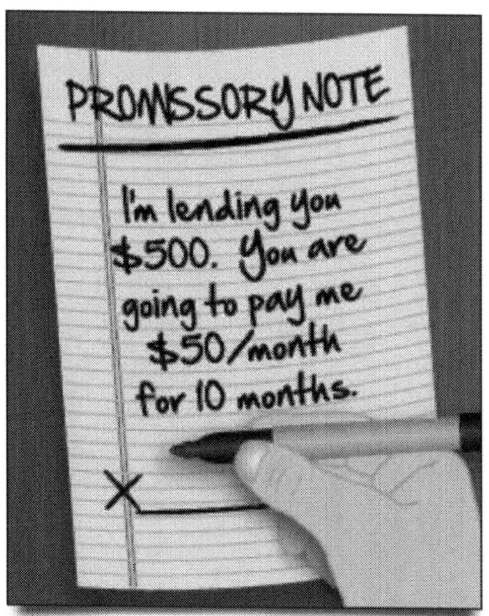

It will also have the 90-day early withdrawal clause mentioned earlier, the minimum return of 6 months, the frequency of payments, if any, before the end of the term, etc.

It's all laid out in about a page and a half. On the other hand, if you go to a bank, they say the same things and a whole lot more in about 50 pages, and it confuses the heck out of you!

The one that my attorney creates is a simple and straightforward promissory note.

And again, my real estate attorney is preparing these documents based on the conditions I provide them from my discussion with my private lender.

I'm not creating this document, nor do I have any interest in creating this. I want to make sure it is all handled professionally, with a licensed attorney taking care of the details.

And it won't cost you a dime since I'm paying for everything!

The Deed of Trust

Next, we have the Deed of Trust, or what most people know as the Mortgage.

So, what is the Deed of Trust?

Well, this is the document that ties the private money to the property. This is the same thing that the banks do to secure the money they lend to the property.

This is the document that allows them to legally foreclose on you if you can't make the payments on the property for some outstanding reason.

It should include things like how much money was borrowed, who's the borrower, who's the lender, the legal description of the property, etc.

So, what's the difference between a Promissory Note and a Deed of Trust?

Think of it this way. A Promissory Note is like an IOU. Like, I promise to pay you back this much money.

A Deed of Trust is what ties the property as security for the loan. It basically says that if you don't pay me back the money in the Promissory Note, I get to take the property as collateral.

Both documents are important to a Private Lender.

I actually have a one-page document where I simply just fill in the blanks for my private lender.

It asks those questions that I just said. All I have to do then is email that one document to my real estate attorney.

That gives them all the information they need to prepare the documents for my private lenders.

When I have a deal ready to close and email that one-page document to my closing attorney, my closing documents are ready to go within 24 business hours.

So again, this document is so easy to use, and it keeps me from spending 20 – 30 minutes on the phone with a paralegal or real estate attorney, giving the terms of a deal every time I do one.

I email it. They get all the information they need and create all the documents for my private lenders. It's like magic!

So, that's the promissory note and the deed of trust or the mortgage. Now, let's move on to the insurance policy.

The Insurance (Hazard) Policy

I have *insurance* on all the properties I work on, especially when I'm buying properties in tornado or hurricane-prone locations.

In September of 2018, Hurricane Florence came and went through the east coast and caused damage to hundreds, if not thousands, of houses!

And then, about a month later, Hurricane Michael hit the same area again with a ton of rain! If you didn't have insurance on your properties... I don't even want to think about it!

In order to protect my private lenders, they are named as additionally insured on the **Hazard Insurance** as the mortgagee on the policy.

If anything were to happen to the house or in the case of a total loss... If the house burns down, or there's hail, or whatever, I can still get my and my private lender's investment back, as long as it is covered under the policy.

The Title Policy

And finally, we've got the title policy or title insurance. Title insurance protects me, the owner, and my private lenders against loss or damage occurring from liens, encumbrances, or defects in the title or actual ownership of a property. This is pretty standard for any lender, including when you use banks and credit unions.

That's it. So, the 5 documents that the lender gets at closing again are as follows:

1. The CMA or BPO
2. The Promissory Note
3. The Deed of Trust (Mortgage)
4. The Insurance (Hazard) Policy
5. The Title Policy

And remember! I don't prepare these documents. My real estate attorney is who prepares these documents!

Every State has its own laws and regulations, and I'm not trained, licensed, or paid enough to stay on top of each, and every law and regulation like a local attorney is.

It's my job to find a licensed professional and pay them to draw up these documents for my safety, as well as the safety of my private lenders.

"A year from now you'll wish you would have started today."

-- Karen Lamb

How Do We Move Forward

I hope you've enjoyed reading this book. In addition, I hope that you've learned a lot about private lending and all its benefits. But, more importantly, I hope you can now recognize the difference between an investor using a proven system to minimize your risk while giving you high returns versus an investor who just wants money to do a deal.

When you work with an investor, who follows the strategies in this book and provides you with the documentation listed within, you'll be able to invest with low risk and get high returns.

As mentioned earlier, this is not a get-rich-quick scheme. The banks have done this for hundreds of years to build a lasting legacy.

There's no magic here.

It's pretty straightforward as long as you follow the guidelines mentioned in this book. Slow and steady wins the race.

So, how do we move forward from here?

Well, it's very simple. We'll want to have a one-on-one conversation, and I'll answer any confidential, non-confidential, or private questions you might have.

Again, if you have any retirement funds of any kind, you'll want to make sure that it's in a self-directed IRA, or I can introduce you to the company I currently use, which has been absolutely fantastic!

They understand and work with thousands of real estate investors and private lenders across the country and are fully approved by the IRS as a third-party custodian.

And at that end of our conversation, when you're ready to move forward with me, you'll just give me a verbal pledge that you've got however much money you have to invest with.

In addition, I'll need to know what kind of funds they are – whether they are retirement funds, investment capital, or even arbitrage funds.

And once we know that information, and you get all set up and are ready to go, I'll find a deal we can do together just as soon as possible.

I'll get it under contract. And then, we'll schedule a closing with the Real Estate Attorney.

And then watch the results! I'm looking forward to working with you as my next private lender!

Yours truly,
Todd Corbin

You Can Be The Bank

Private Lending Summary & F.A.Q.

What does it mean to become one of my Private Lenders?

When I desire to borrow money by offering the property as collateral, I give my Private Lender an opportunity to make the loan... and earn high interest rates that are up to 14 times as much as the rates you can get on bank CDs or other traditional resources.

How will I be using your money?

As a professional real estate investor, I need to fund new purchases, sometimes do renovations and fix up properties... plus cover the other costs associated with buying and selling houses. For properties I already own and manage, there are times when I want to convert some of the equity into cash - without selling the property. I do this by doing a "cash-out refinance" using a private lender instead of a bank. This cash may be used to fund my house buying business, pay off other real estate notes that come due, or handle other cash needs.

Why don't you go to banks or mortgage lenders?

Banks and other lenders require applications, approvals and must follow guidelines imposed by the banking industry. Plus, there are limits to the number of loans they can make to any one company or investor. On top of that, the time it takes for their approval process is never certain. I can move much faster without these limitations by using Private Lenders. That allows me to negotiate more profitable deals while offering homeowners a quick and easy sale without new loan or deal breaking contingencies.

How can I afford to pay such high rates?

I make my money by providing valuable services to sellers, buyers, renters and Private Lenders. By cutting out the middlemen, I can avoid the costs normally paid out for real estate commissions, mortgage broker fees, loan fees and property management fees. I also know how to sell homes at a full appraised value and avoid making price concessions. I can get a home occupied fast to avoid holding costs, and I know how to fix up and maintain properties for less money than most people pay.

I calculate my offers on properties so that buyers and sellers get a great deal. At the same time a minimum profit of $30,000 to $50,000 is earned between the time of purchase and sale. I won't just buy a property unless it makes sense for everyone involved. The deal has "to work" for all parties.

How do I help sellers?

A lot of sellers today are having trouble finding a buyer. And there are typically a lot of hassles sellers must endure to get their home sold. Using a long-term investing approach, I can offer sellers an attractive price, close or take possession whenever they want... and give them an opportunity to avoid all the hassles of selling a house.

How do I help buyers?

I offer several great programs and unique opportunities for buyers. This includes an owner financing program, down payment assistance program and a sweat equity program. Buyers today are finding it more and more difficult to qualify for loans. These programs help buyers get into a home they want to purchase quickly... allowing them to start building equity for the future and helping them avoid throwing their money away on rent.

Am I concerned about housing prices going down today?

> No. We're prepared to hold properties for 2 to 3 years. That way we're not as concerned about short term price fluctuations in home prices as other investors are. Most of our investing plans are determined by the income we expect the property to produce now and in the future.

What interest rate do you pay?

> That depends on the deal at hand, what works for you, and what works for me. It will be much higher than any CD or traditional investment. It also depends on the current market rates.

How long will my investment funds be tied up?

> Most of my private loans are set up on a 3, 4, or 5-year term. However, it depends on what the Private Lender wants and needs... and what the deal is. So, depending on our plan for the property, we might be able to offer you a shorter term... or we may ask if you're willing to commit to a longer term plan. Regardless, you'll always decide what term works best for you.

What if I commit to a longer term and then need my money sooner?

> My policy is to pay off (or replace) any Private Lender who requests an early payoff whenever possible. Sometimes a partial early payoff meets the lender's needs, allowing the rest of their money to continue to earn the high rates. I ask you to give me advance notice, preferably 90 days, so we can do whatever we can to meet your request. I would attempt to meet such a request by refinancing the property, selling the property, or most likely, having another one of my Private Lenders take over your position.

Will I earn interest for the entire term of the note?

> Your interest is fixed and locked in for as long as the note is out. However, I may sell or refinance the property before the full term is up. You'll always earn your note interest until it's paid in full. But I do have the right to pay off the note early.

What if you pay me off only a month after I invest?

I understand you might be liquidating investments or foregoing another investment program to get a high rate of return. Therefore, I agree in writing, you'll receive a minimum of 6 months of interest. So, if I need to pay you off sooner than expected, I would either move your mortgage to another property by substituting the collateral, or pay you off in full including a minimum of 6 months of interest earned.

Will I receive monthly payments?

Most of my Private Lenders prefer letting the interest accrue and getting a big check when the property cashes out. A few Private Lenders prefer payments. These lenders are usually retired and have cash flow needs.

What is My minimum investment?

My "First Position Private Lenders" would usually need a minimum available to invest of $100,000 for most deals. However, there are some deals that come along now and then where a lower amount could be accepted. My "Second Position Private Lenders" would usually need a minimum of $25,000.

Is your investment program insured by the government?

> No. There is no government backed guarantee on these real estate notes. However, your protection and security is the amount of equity in the property that secures the note. Usually, I will not allow my Private Lenders to loan more than 75% (although I will go up to 85%) of the value of the property securing the note. That way, the Private Lenders always have at least a 25% "Equity Cushion" in the property.

Has the IRS approved using retirement accounts?

> YES! The IRS does establish guidelines that must be followed in order for a Retirement Account (IRA) to invest in real estate notes tax deferred or tax free. You'll need the services of a company approved by the IRS to act as your custodian to invest your retirement funds. We have been very pleased with our current IRA company, and we'll be glad to answer questions about it.

What kind of fees are there for set up of the IRA, transfers in and out to secure the property and receive payments? Are there basic custodial fees and if so, what are they?

> Different companies have different fees. If you are using the company I recommend, there is a flat annual management fee for a year based on the size of your account. There will be a small transaction fee for each deal. This is less than most regular retirement accounts. Some companies charge an expedited fee to have things move along quickly. My company moves things within 48 hours and doesn't charge an expedited fee.

How do I know if there's enough value or equity in the property to sufficiently protect my investment?

> I usually do not borrow more than 75% of the value of a property using Private Lender money. That leaves at least a 25% cushion of equity. You will receive full details on the value, status and condition of the property whenever I present you with an opportunity to lend.

Do you provide title insurance?

> Absolutely! I never buy a property without title insurance. However, if I am refinancing a property, there would be no need for a new title policy.

Are there any Upfront Costs?

I pay for all closing costs, so your entire investment goes to work for you. I will pay for the closing real estate attorney, document prep fees, notary fees, overnight mail fees, and recording costs. There are no charges nor fees whatsoever incurred by you.

What happens if the property burns down?

A valid hazard insurance policy is always in place to protect against casualties. You'll be named as a mortgagee. Insurance distributions would be used to rebuild or repair the property, or used to pay you off.

Will my money be pooled with other investors?

No. Your funds will fund one real estate note secured by a Deed of Trust or Mortgage on a property with sufficient equity as protection.

What is a junior lien or second mortgage?

It's a loan secured by real estate that is positioned behind a senior mortgage or first mortgage.

What kinds of documents and paperwork will I receive?

> Your closing package should include: Original Promissory Note, Copy of the Deed of Trust or Mortgage, Copy of Property Insurance Binder naming you as the mortgagee, a Title Insurance Policy insuring you against any title problems, and an Appraisal or BPO of the property.

If you default and don't keep your promises, how am I protected?

> In this unlikely event, I would simply transfer ownership of the property to you. You would be owning the property at 75% of its value, therefore making it easy for a quick sale at a profit. Plus, you have all the legal rights of a secured lender.

If you sell the property on a "Lease/Option Basis," and the "tenant/buyers" trash the property, what happens?

> It's my responsibility to protect the property as well as to protect your collateral. My crew would take care of any repairs, and you never have to get involved.

How do I get started becoming one of your Private Lenders?

> Once I know how much you want to invest at a high rate of return, when those funds will be available, and how long of a term you're willing to go, I will begin looking for a deal for you. When I select one that meets your goals and investment objectives, you will receive all the details on the property.

Would you possibly work with other people I know that might be interested in being a Private Lender?

> It's my policy to work with people I already have an existing relationship with and with folks they refer. In other words, I work with folks "By Referral Only." You can certainly refer potential lenders to me. I'll explain the program and learn about their investment objectives and goals. Once I get to know them, there is a possibility they can also become one of my Private Lenders.

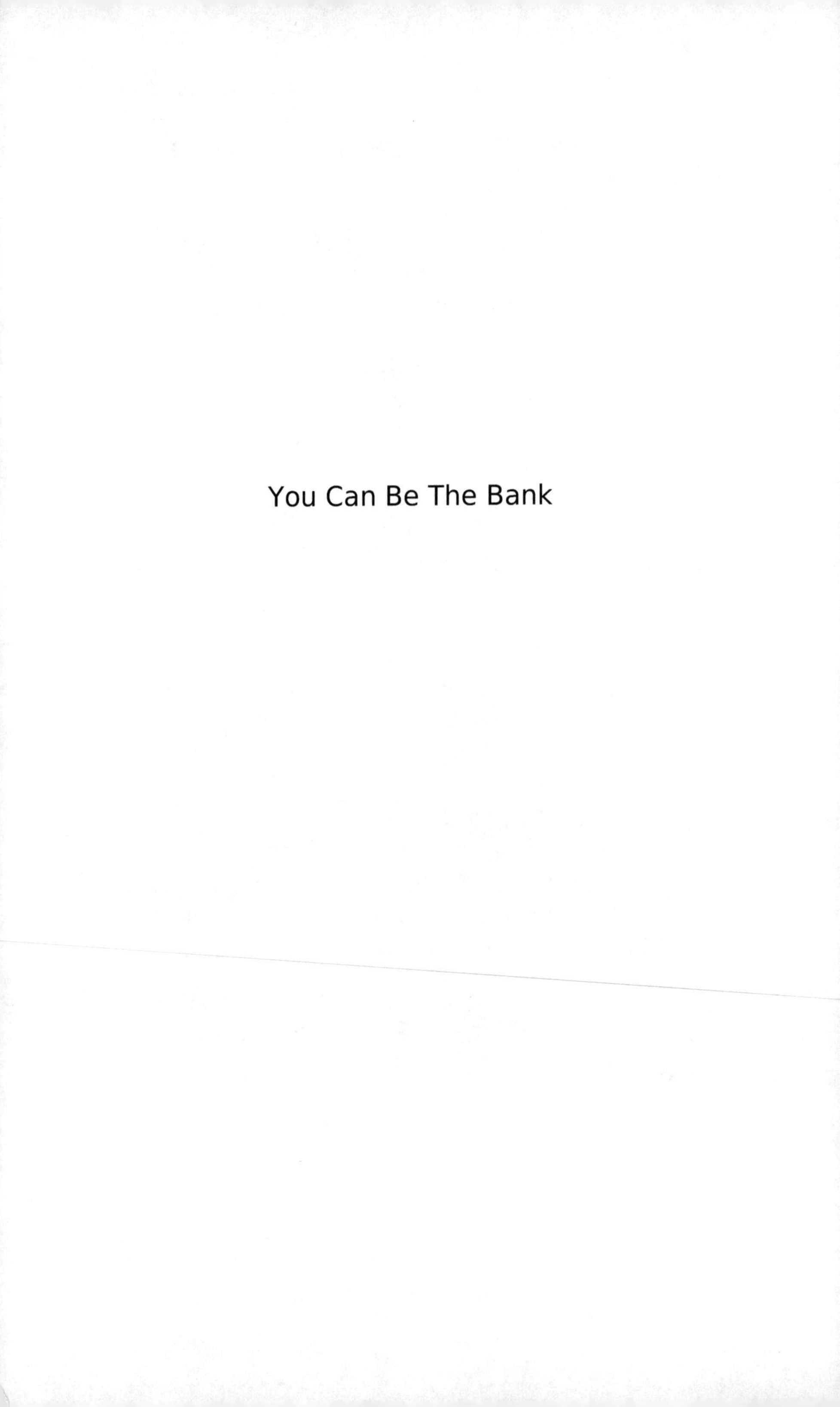

You Can Be The Bank

In Case You Missed It... Free! – Special Bonus Gift

As my way of saying thank you for taking an active role in your success education, I have made an additional bonus gift available to you worth over $97, and it's yours absolutely free for picking up You Can Be The Bank!

Visit my special book bonus website and get your special report called How To Use Your Self-Directed IRA To Unlock Unlimited Tax-Free or Tax-Deferred Earnings.

This special report will walk you through step-by-step on how to become a private lender using your Traditional or ROTH IRA and multiply your earnings safely and securely.

Get it here:
https://integrityinvestsolutions.com/#freereport

As an added bonus, when you get the report, I'll send you an invitation to attend Jay Conner's upcoming 3-Day Private Money Conference priced at $2,997 per person.

When you attend, you'll learn exactly what I do and why I do it. You'll see for yourself how safe and secure your money will be when you work with me as a private lender. Jay's attorney will be at this event along with some of his existing private lenders! You will be able to see exactly how private lending works and how you can earn money on your money safely and securely. As my guest, the ticket price of $2,997 is waived, and you can now attend for only a $97 registration fee for both YOU and a guest!

Thank you and I hope you enjoyed reading the book!

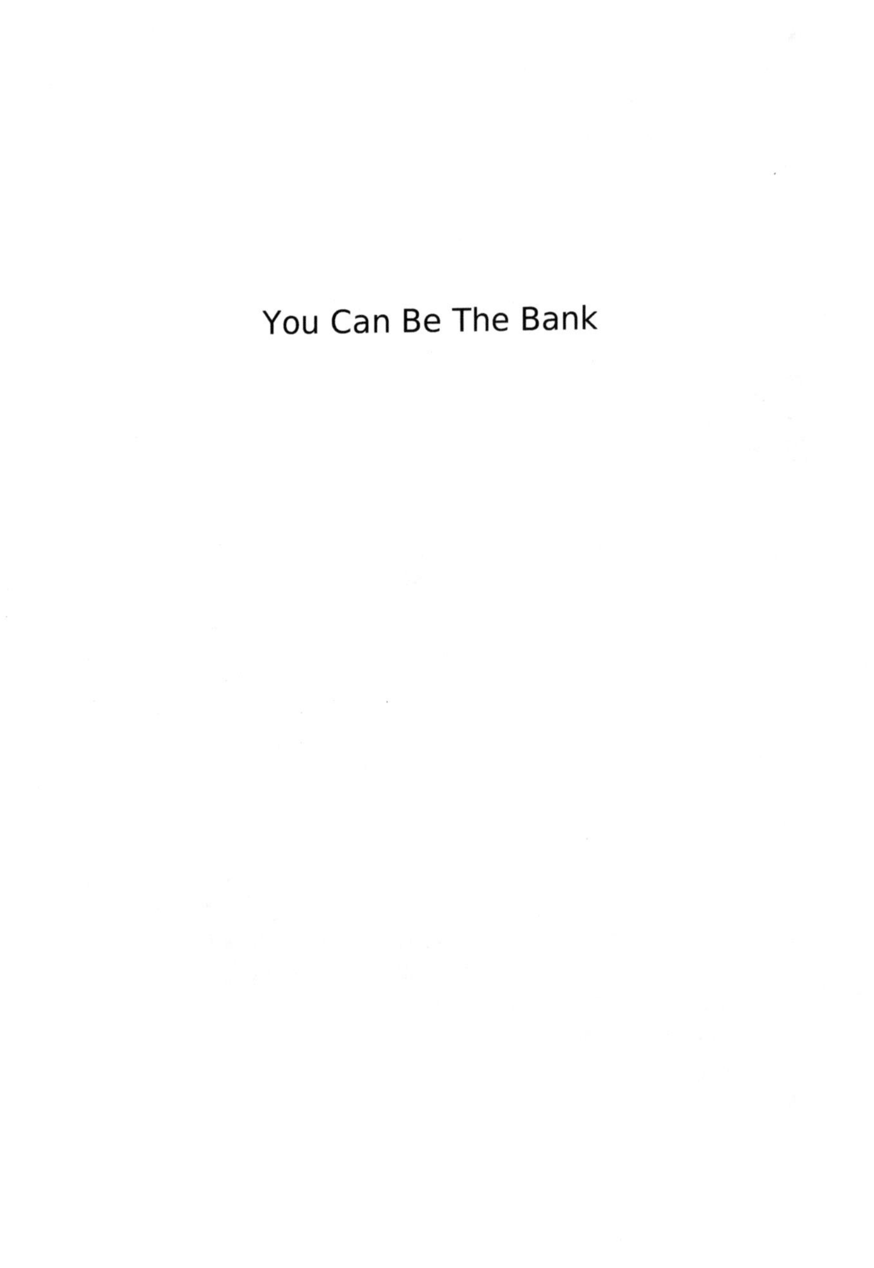

You Can Be The Bank

ABOUT THE AUTHOR

Todd Corbin grew up in the Midwest, but has lived in several regions of the country, as well as overseas. Having lived in so many places and traveled extensively worldwide, he has a large network of people that know and love him and have been impacted by his life.

He loves making a difference in the lives of others and has spent his entire adult life doing that. He is a former high school teacher, worship leader, missionary, youth worker, team leader, and now entrepreneur and author.

When he was introduced to the world of real estate investing, he saw this as still another way he could help many more people: potential investors, distressed homeowners, and homebuyers that don't yet qualify for a mortgage.

Todd and his wife, Liana, became private lenders in 2022, and have seen incredible results.

With this book, Todd wants to teach you how easily you too can transform your financial stability through private lending.

Thank You For Reading
You Can Be The Bank!

Made in the USA
Columbia, SC
13 October 2023

24007972R00163